Endpapers and page 1: *Tabby Cat and
Kittens*; 2–3, *British Shorthairs*, (left)
Silver Tabby, (right) *Silver Spotted*; 4–5,
Seal Point Siamese; 6–7, *Cameo Cat*.

Beautiful
CATS

Beautiful
CATS

Howard Loxton

Cathay Books

Contents

First published in Great Britain in 1980 by
Octopus Books Limited

This edition published in 1988 by
Cathay Books
Michelin House
81 Fulham Road
London SW3 6RB

ISBN 0 86178 539 8

Printed and bound in Hong Kong

Introduction

It is difficult, perhaps, to think of the furry bundle sleeping by the fire or purring gently on your lap as a fierce predator, and a close relative of the lion of the African plain and the tiger of the Indian forests. Yet, if you watch a family of lion cubs at play they are very like a litter of kittens; if you see a tabby cat hunting through the bushes it is not so difficult to picture a miniature tiger with its flashing eyes and sinuous stalk.

The cat family had evolved in a recognizable form many million years ago and were so efficiently developed that they have changed very little, much less, for instance, than the dog, although their association with man has been, in terms of their development, a very recent one.

Several different types have appeared over the centuries: the sleek 'oriental' cats which may have originated in the east, the familiar short-haired European cats and the long-haired ones which at some point appeared in the middle-east, but it was not until the last century that cat fanciers began to develop the breeds we know today.

There are now more than 100 different breeds recognized around the world and an infinite number of variations among mongrel cats but although they may have superficial differences of coat and pattern they are much more alike than breeds of dog which were usually man-created to emphasize some inherent skill or work potential. The cat has only been expected to fulfil one working role – to be an efficient vermin catcher – and human interference has effected only superficial changes in appearance. Alley-cat or show champion with a mile-long pedigree, a cat is a cat: graceful and clever, lively and cunning, capable of being an affectionate friend and a perfect pet. While we may have forced our pets to live in a world where they are dependent upon us, they have not become our property; indeed, many cat owners would admit that their cat 'owns' them!

The cat's natural instincts have been little modified by living with man. It will accept the food, shelter and attention we provide – and which, of course, we owe it since we have taken it out of the circumstances where it could happily provide for itself; it may be prepared to live by certain rules we make, provided they do not conflict too strongly with its basic needs: but it will still live like a cat. To keep it happy and healthy and to obtain the greatest pleasure from its company we must keep that in mind and never adopt an anthropomorphic attitude towards it.

Every cat is an individual and some breeds do have clear characteristics, as this book explains; but, whatever its type or colour, it will share the same feline instincts and feline needs. This book will tell you some of its history, advise you how to choose a cat, describe its physical and sensual capabilities, and discuss its needs. It will help you to understand your cat better and care for it in the way that it requires, so that you may spend many happy years together.

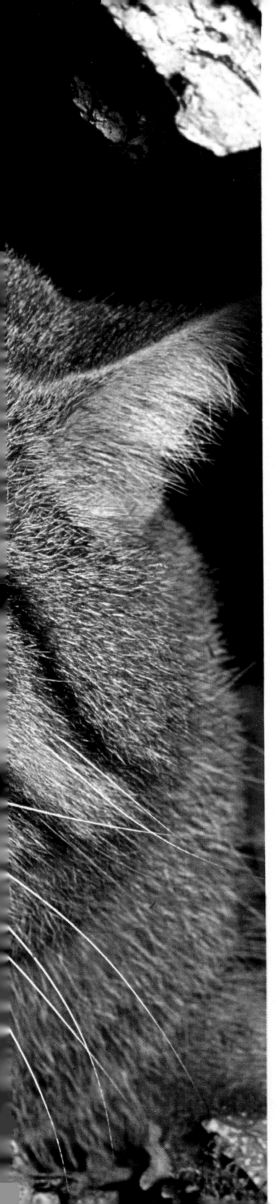

How the cat became a pet

'A home without a cat, and a well-fed, well-petted and properly revered cat, may be a perfect home, perhaps, but how can it prove its title?' so wrote American Mark Twain, and I agree: a house without a cat would not feel like home to me. The cat is one of the more recent of the animals which man has domesticated, and settled into its place by the fireside long after the dog had become man's companion and cattle, sheep and goats had come under his control. Dogs hunted with man for centuries before the first appearance of a cat in the human entourage.

Perhaps the reason lies in man's own history: the dog is a pack animal, whereas the cat hunts alone, so it had nothing to gain by throwing in its lot with the prehistoric hunter. When man became a herdsman, following his flocks in search of fresh pasture, there was no attraction for the territory-loving cat, nor advantage to the humans. But when man stopped wandering to raise crops, made a settled home and began to store his grain, there was something to be gained from an association, for grain attracted mice and rats. Although there is no historical record of the cat's domestication, many of the myths and fables about the creation of the cat emphasize its rodent-catching skill. We can imagine that wild cats, discovering large numbers of rats and mice around the grain stores of ancient peoples, found these places easier hunting grounds than the plains and forests, and the shelter and warmth of human habitations more comfortable than a rocky hole or sandy hollow. At the same time man recognized and welcomed this ally against vermin. It is surely no coincidence that the earliest known human records of cats are wall paintings in ancient Egypt, a land which was dependent upon the grain harvest from the valley of the Nile.

The earliest Egyptian cat painting is a mural in a tomb dating from about 2600 BC. It shows a cat wearing a collar, but that is not proof than it was domesticated. Ancient Chinese paintings of cats have also been discovered, dating from about 500 years later, but these, too, could be of wild cats. However, we know for

Left: *The European Wild Cat looks very like a domestic tabby.*

Below: *The African Wild Cat was probably the species first domesticated in Egypt where it was shown in wall paintings.*

The mummies of Bubastis

The Egyptians thought so highly of their cats that they mummified their bodies and placed them in beautifully woven wrappings or bronze caskets. Many thousands of cats were taken to the cult centre of Bubastis for burial, and nineteenth-century Egyptologists discovered more than 300,000 of them laid upon tiered shelves in the tunnels of a subterranean cemetery.

Kittens were often simply dipped in a solution of preservative chemicals and then wrapped in linen. Their remains have consequently survived only as bundles of dust and fragmented bones.

Adult cats were treated more elaborately with chemicals, oils and spices, then (if the owner could afford it) carefully and elaborately wrapped. The body was arranged with the rear legs placed in a sitting posture, the front paws were stretched straight down and the tail was curled forward to lie against the belly. In this position the cat was wound in a sheet of linen and then wrapped in a cylindrical covering of plaited ribbons in two colours, probably to represent the pattern of the fur. A mask made from papyrus paper covered the head, with linen discs sewn on and coloured to represent the eyes, and nostrils and upright ears were fashioned from palm-leaf fronds.

The mummy was then placed in a funerary box of wood or bronze which was often shaped like a seated cat. The wooden ones were painted and sometimes had bronze heads, or heads painted to suggest bronze. Kittens in particular were sometimes encased in bronze in a box often surmounted by a figure of a cat. One such find was only three inches long, and must have been made for a kitten that died at birth. This particular one is guarded by four bronze kittens.

What happened to those thousands of burials at Bubastis? Apart from the ones in the British Museum and other collections which represent only a handful of the whole, they were destroyed: heads were slashed off and the contents spread as manure for local crops, and two tons were pulverised and shipped as fertilizer to England during the nineteenth century.

certain that by 2000 BC cats were already the object of a well-established religious cult in Egypt, and there is solid evidence that by 200 years later they were domesticated in the modern sense.

The Egyptians venerated a number of their gods and goddesses in feline form, including the great Sun God, Ra, Mafdet (presented as a snake-killing cat) and the cat-headed Bast. At the cult centre for Bast, the city of Bubastis on the Lower Nile, a great temple was built. In its courtyard lived the shrine's own cats, which were carefully watched by the priests for any message from the goddess which their behaviour might reveal.

Many thousands of devotees flocked to Bubastis each year on the occasion of the great festival of Bast. They sailed down the Nile in gaily-decked boats, with music and ribaldry echoing across the water. Bast was a goddess of fertility, and the celebration of her rites reached an orgiastic fervour that shocked visitors in later centuries, but her popularity was undiminished and her cult flourished right into the Christian era, when it was suppressed by the Byzantine emperor Theodosius in AD 392. Her worship lasted longer than the Christian Church has so far existed.

Ancient Egyptian laws severely punished anyone who deliberately harmed a cat, and such laws were an expression of popular feeling, which held the cat in high regard. When a Persian army advanced upon an Egyptian city in 500 BC it is said that the inhabitants offered no resistance because each Persian soldier carried before him a cat taken from the surrounding countryside and the Egyptians would not fight for fear of harming the sacred animals.

Revered though they were, Egyptian domestic cats were also pets and working animals. In addition to guarding grain they possibly helped to rid the household of snakes; the Sun God Ra, in his cat form, was thought daily to overcome the darkness in the form of a snake, and this symbolic act perhaps reflected real life, for there are recorded instances of cats killing snakes. It is possible that the Egyptians also used their cats as retrievers, although they may simply have been used for flushing out the fowl. A mural painting from a Theban tomb shows a fowling party in a boat and a cat in the rushes holding down one bird whilst firmly gripping another in its mouth.

The Egyptians may have believed that the domestication of the cat gave them some advantage over other nations, for the export of cats was strictly forbidden, but cats were smuggled overseas and began to appear in Greece and Italy. Cats were featured on Greek coins, in vase paintings and on funeral monuments, but achieved no great importance. However in Roman times the growing fashion for exotic religions, including the cult of Bast, increased the cat's appeal. Its value as a rodent killer must have been known, although it is not until the fourth century AD that we find the agriculturalist Palladius recommending the use of cats to protect gardens from mice and moles. As Rome spread her dominion across the known world we can imagine that the cat followed in the wake of her armies, for cat remains have been found in Britain and other outposts of the Empire in situations which suggest that they were domestic animals. The Romans identified the goddess Bast with their Diana, moon goddess and huntress, and the cat became her animal. It was also closely linked with the Nordic goddess Freya. Its symbolic connection with fertility gave it a magic role in many countries, including its sacrifice at the end of the harvest in some places. In France and Germany cats may have been eaten ritually when the harvest started. In China the farmers worshipped a fertility god, Li Chou, in cat form and offered sacrifices to the cats when the reaping ended in an orgiastic festival.

Right: *The European Wild Cat is usually larger than a domestic cat and has a rounded tail tip.*

As Christianity sought to re-establish itself in Europe after the pagan times which followed the fall of the Roman Empire, a strange dual attitude developed. On the one hand, laws in countries as far apart as Wales and Germany protected cats; they were the approved companions for English nuns, and a cat accompanied Pope Gregory the Great when he retired to secular life. On the other hand they were also considered to be agents of the devil; the Roman Diana (with her cat) became Hecate, queen of the night and chief of witches, and since the Church condemned all the surviving ancient religions as devil-worship the cat was designated Satan's animal. Yet, in Provence, on Corpus Christi day, in a ceremony redolent of the pagan rituals, a cat was wrapped up like a baby and burned at noon, an echo of sun worship and fertility offering. Was the cat also supposed to represent the sacrifice of Christ? Elsewhere, in Metz and Paris, for example, cats were burned publicly as a symbolic destruction of the evil which they represented through their association with paganism and the devil.

The character of the cat was further blackened when the Church sought to show the heresy of those Christian groups which disagreed with the official Roman dogma or which the establishment saw as a threat. The Cathars, in southern France, and the Waldensians, in Germany, were accused of worshipping the devil in the form of a cat, and a century later the evidence against the Order of Knights Templar, which led to its disbanding, included charges that they indulged in satanic rites which involved a black cat.

The persecution of the cat made it possible for the rats of Europe to multiply unchecked and allowed the rapid spread of the Black Death and other terrible plagues.

The cat had its enemies but it also had many friends, even through the darkest days of persecution, from the simple monk of the early Irish church, who compared the way his cat hunted mice to the way he spent the night hunting words as he bent over his writing desk, to the grandiloquent and powerful Cardinal Richelieu who, in the seventeenth century, kept 14 cats, Cardinal Wolsey, Henry VIII's once-favoured Chancellor, Popes

Gregory III and Leo XII were other churchmen who loved cats. Perhaps in their celibate existence they turned to their cats for loving companionship. Cats also earned a place in many more lowly households. Shakespeare called them 'harmless' and 'necessary' and in England there was never the wholesale condemnation seen on the Continent, although there was plenty of cruelty: for instance, in a demonstration against the Pope at the coronation of Elizabeth I, six cats were placed inside an effigy of the pontiff so that as it burned their cries would sound like 'the language of devils' inside His Holiness. During the Great Plague in 1665 Londoners made the mistake of

Above: *Friendly pet or witch's familiar? It has been claimed that the devil himself would take the form of a black cat.*

killing their cats and dogs as suspected carriers of the disease, when they were in fact the best means of exterminating the rats which were, of course, the real hosts of the deadly plague-carrying flea.

A cat, an ideal companion for the poor and lonely, can hunt and forage for itself when food is short; one cat used to bring in pigeons to supplement the diet of a prisoner in the Tower of London. It provided the poor man with warmth on cold nights and its contented purring and displays of affection gave reassurance and comfort to its adopted master when the rest of the world seemed not to care. Yet there could be danger if a person became too close to his pet. Harmless and necessary as Shakespeare's contemporaries might

agree the cat to be, their fears and superstitions led them to misinterpret the close bond between human and pet, towards the end of the reign of Elizabeth I and at the beginning of that of her successor, James I of England (VI of Scotland), many people firmly believed in magic and witchcraft. Witches were hunted and even an old woman with a pet cat might come under suspicion. King James himself was fascinated by the super-natural. He wrote a book about it called *Daemonologie* and took a personal interest in witchcraft investigations. There was a similar paranoia on the Continent.

In Europe it was generally believed that witches, warlocks and Satan himself had the power to take the form of animals. There are many folk stories in which this happens and the animal form was often that of a cat. In Britain it was thought that witches were frequently linked with the devil by 'familiars', (lesser devils who acted as servants to the witch or warlock), which frequently took animal form. They might be dogs, toads, rabbits – almost any creature, not necessarily cats – but records of the trials of witches include many references to cat familiars and it is the cat which has remained associated with witches in the popular imagination to this day.

Evidence offered against witches and their 'confessions' frequently refer to the use of the rubbing of the cat with the clothing or possessions of the supposed 'victim' of the witch's spells and of strange intimacies between witch and familiar. Perhaps in an age when animals were not particularly highly regarded or well cared for, most people could not tell one black cat from another, particularly if the owner called it by the same name: how else can one explain the statement in a Yorkshire trial that a witch had an attendant spirit 'in the shape of a great black cat called Gibbe, which hath attended her now above forty years'?

The peak of the witch persecution mania in Britain came in the middle of the seventeenth century when Matthew Hopkins set himself up as the Witch Finder General of England.

Right: *Puss-in-Boots is one of the best-known characters in the many legends and fairy stories featuring cats.*

SONGS FOR CHILDREN

WORDS BY
EDWARD LEAR, ESQ^R   N° 5, THE OWL & THE PUSSY-CAT.   MUSIC BY
M^{RS} J. WORTHINGTON BLISS.
(MISS LINDSAY.)

ENT.STA.HALL.   London,   PRICE 3/6
LAMBORN COCK, 63, NEW BOND STREET.

N° 1 THE ROBIN   N° 4 THE FOX & THE HEN
   2 THE DUCK   5 THE OWL & THE PUSSY-CAT
   3 THE CUCKOO   6 M^{RS} BLUEBOTTLE FLY

Left: *Edward Lear's cat who 'went to sea in a beautiful pea-green boat' became an all-time nursery favourite.*

Right: *Sentimental studies such as this one dated 1887, were extremely popular in Victorian times.*

that of *Puss-in-Boots*, which had already been told in classic form by the French writer Charles Perrault, and the English tale of *Dick Whittington*. In France there was a traditional belief in magician cats, known as *matagots*, who would bring prosperity to a home where they were loved and well looked after, and the story of Whittington (a real Mayor of London), who gained his fortune when his cat cleared all the rats from the island of an oriental potentate, is an echo of much earlier tales from several parts of the world.

In Germany in 1747 cats were once again being persecuted by the Church but for their skill as hunters, not for any religious reason. The Archbishop of Cologne issued a decree that because 'the constant roaming of cats in field and forest has resulted in the snatching and consuming of young hares and partridges, to the detriment of the hunt' all subjects of the archbishopric, regardless of rank, were 'to cut the ears of all cats in their possession right back to the head, thereby hindering the cats from roaming and poaching in the field'. There were to be monthly inspections to see that the order was carried out, with a large fine for any contravention.

The eighteenth century still saw a great deal of cruelty to animals. One of Hogarth's engravings shows a cat being savaged by a dog for human entertainment, two cats being strung up from a post and another, with two balloons attached, being flung from an attic window. Nevertheless, a more responsible attitude with animals seems to have been developing among many people, with writers and artists paying more attention to the animals themselves where previously they mainly found a place as a symbol or metaphor. Some of the cat enthusiasts went too far: John Rich, manager of the Theatre Royal, Drury Lane and first presenter of *The Beggar's Opera*, was one example. He surrounded himself with cats – there were at least 27 present on one occasion when one of his actresses tried to count them.

In one year alone he sent more than 200 'witches' to their deaths. Many confessed that they had had dealings with the devil, but often only under torture, and as many of them were psychologically disturbed they may have come to believe the accusations brought against them. Nevertheless there were sceptics, including King James himself, whose interest may have been a reason for the great number of prosecutions but who realized that many were misguided and was eager to expose counterfeit witchcraft and to prevent wrongful prosecution. At the very peak of Hopkins' activities a Puritan preacher, John Paul, published a collection of sermons on witchcraft in which he declared that 'every old woman with a wrinkled face, a hairy lip, a squint eye, a spindle in her hand, and a cat or dog by her side, is not only suspected but pronounced a witch'.

The witch-hunting mania did not remain confined to Europe. The religious zealots among the early emigrants to America took their beliefs and fears with them. The most famous American witchcraft trials took place in the New England colonies in 1692 at Salem, Massachusetts. Among the evidence given was the incident of a cat which, the witness claimed, came in through a window the night after one of the defendants had threatened that a 'she devil would shortly fetch him away'. The cat jumped upon him, gripping his throat, but when he called on the names of the Trinity it released him and 'flew out of the window'.

The last witch trial in England took place in 1712, that in Scotland 10 years later: in both trials a cat was named as the witch's familiar. By this time the cat was being presented as a benevolent creature in stories like

The British have gained a reputation as animal-lovers, and it was the British Parliament which, in 1822, passed the first legislation protecting animals, although initially it applied only to cattle and beasts of burden. Two years later, at a meeting of animal-lovers held in London, a Society for the Prevention of Cruelty to Animals was established.

For centuries men had considered animals largely dispensable, and everyone had the right to treat their animals (and their children) as they wished. Jeremy Bentham, the English lawyer and philosopher, was one of the first to suggest that animals, too, had rights, and others supported his view. In 1840 Queen Victoria gave the SPCA her patronage and the prefix Royal. In 1849 another Act of Parliament extended legal protection to all domestic animals. A change in the law does not necessarily effect a change in human beings and, since its formation, the RSPCA has actively protected animals, taking to court nearly 1,000 cases each year and investigating perhaps twenty times as many, even in our supposedly more enlightened times.

In 1866 the American SPCA was formed, followed by other animal protection societies across the world. At the same time veterinary medicine advanced with speed. In 1844, when the Royal College of Veterinary Surgeons was incorporated by Royal Charter, interest centred largely upon the horse. Veterinary knowledge has expanded amazingly, research keeping pace with much human medicine: it should be remembered that experiments on animals, however distressing, often provide means of helping animals as well as humans. The majority of today's vets with urban practices cater largely for small mammals, and for any pet owner who cannot afford to pay private veterinary bills the welfare societies, such as the People's Dispensary for Sick Animals and the Blue Cross, provide free medical services.

The cat's position in law varies from one country to another and from State to State in America. In Britain, cats are classified as wild animals and do not have to be licensed or taxed, but in some parts of the United States a licence is required and local law in Saddle Brook, New Jersey, for

The origin of the cat

Several stories date the creation of the cat at the time of the Flood. In one of them, when the animals had all been led into the Ark, Noah, afraid that the mouse and rat would eat all the grain aboard, asked for it to be protected. In answer to his prayer the lion sneezed and from his nostrils sprang a pair of cats.

Another version tells how Noah shepherded all the animals into the Ark and then all his family, except his wife.

'Come in,' he said to her.

'No,' she obstinately refused.

Noah began to get angry for the waters were beginning to rise.

'Oh, you devil, come in,' he said.

That was just what the devil had been waiting for. He knew that Noah would not let him in the Ark but now he had been given an invitation and the devil took advantage of it, but he did not intend to take any risks so he turned himself into a mouse.

As soon as they set sail the devil set to work gnawing at the planks of the Ark to make a hole and drown all God's creatures. Noah caught him at his wickedness and threw a fur glove at him. Immediately the glove turned into a cat and at one and the same moment the cat had siezed the mouse and held it firmly in its mouth.

However, there had to be peace in the Ark so Noah seized the cat, the mouse still in its mouth, and flung it out into the water. The cat swam back to the Ark and managed to clamber up the side and find space to stretch out and dry on the doorstep. There it stayed until the water subsided and that is where you will often find it today, lying on your doorstep, basking in the sun.

In an added garnish to this cat-glove tale, another story claims that because the cat ate the mouse the devil made the cat's fur bristle and give off sparks when touched, and made its eyes glisten in the dark – phenomena common to all cats today.

Dogs will almost always accept a subservient role but cats expect a more egalitarian attitude and will stand by what they consider their rights. There are people who deride those who lavish a great deal of affection on their pets, but our need to give affection is one shared by many creatures and does not have to be limited to our own species. Of course, this can be overdone, but if it helps a person to be happy, who has the right to criticize? It was such thoughtless attitudes that labelled the innocent as witches. I personally draw the line at such horrors as dressing up animals (even as a children's game it may not be very pleasant for the animal) or other attitudes which seek to change the animal's essential nature. A cat owner should remember that a cat is a cat and allow it to live in the way that suits its nature.

People often criticize the money spent upon pets and their consumption of food in a world that has many hungry people. But if that money were not spent on animals would it find its way to humans in need? The food used in the massive pet-food industry is largely meat and grain that would not normally find a market for human consumption in the countries where it is sold. Large parts of the world produce a surplus of food which does not find its way to the hungry millions. Such problems would not be solved by abandoning our pets. What would be the cost, in social terms, to human happiness if we had no pets?

There are still many places where cats earn their keep in their traditional role as rodent controllers: shops, factories, warehouses, offices and docks as well as homes. They are provided for in the official budgets of government institutions, museums, post-offices and ministries. However, most of us choose a cat as a pet because of its inherent appeal rather than its usefulness, and although it may not find much employment as a rodent exterminator it earns its place in our homes for the pleasure, comfort and happiness it brings.

instance, decrees that all cats must wear a collar with a bell. In New York State adults with a hunting licence are permitted to destroy any cat found hunting or killing any bird of a protected species. Because cats are considered wild, and therefore uncontrollable, British owners are not responsible for their cat's behaviour, unless it can be shown that they have deliberately caused it to do something to the detriment of others. However, that does not mean that the cat itself has no rights. Anyone deliberately inflicting pain or injury on or to a cat is liable to be punished and to pay compensation to the animal's owner. Similarly, owners who fail to protect their cats from cruelty, people who put down poison without taking precautions to prevent injury to cats, and any person who carries out an operation on a cat without due care and humanity, are all liable to prosecution.

Today, we probably regard our cats primarily as companions and pets. Few of us now have firm roots in the way that our forefathers did. Social and physical mobility breaks close ties and families fragment as children move away. More and more people find that the family unit shrinks, and we are no longer surrounded by a close community of friends and relations. Home no longer means a wide environment but the private space behind our own front door or the narrow confines of a single room, where we can feel secure, protected from the pressures of the modern world, but there, too, there are many who feel lonely, not just alone. Never before, perhaps, have pets played such an important role in supplying a stable and reassuring focus, a welcoming friend on returning home, a living creature to fuss over and feel responsible for in the absence of a family. At the very least a cat is a creature to boss and complain at (although my cats answer back), at best a sharing companion.

Many people decide to let their children have a cat in the belief that caring for an animal will develop a child's sense of responsibility. For the child it may be much more: warm, comforting and cuddly, returning affection with a purr, with an affection unmixed with reproof or lecture, a cherished friend always happy to join in a game or to share a secret and keep it safe.

Choosing a cat

Why a cat? It is difficult for any of us to know just what it is that makes us choose a cat as a pet, or why we want to keep a pet at all. It is usually a mixture of all sorts of things: companionship, keeping mice away, physical appeal – and that general, inexplicable but delightful pleasure given by animals in the home. There may be practical reasons for a choice: a cat fits more easily into a flat or small house than most breeds of dog, a cat will probably cost less to feed (and probably less to buy), a cat can be house-trained so that it does not have to be taken outside and a cat will usually be less noisy than a dog.

However, many of us have both a cat and a dog and there is nothing more nonsensical than the idea that there are cat people and dog people and that they are mutually exclusive, or that cats and dogs are necessarily antagonistic. On the contrary, many who share a household seem devoted to each other: indeed, companionship for a dog who has to be left alone for long periods in the day may be a very good reason for acquiring a cat.

Working out your own motives for wanting a cat will help you to decide what sort of cat to have. Should it be a

Left: *The appeal of a young kitten is often difficult to resist! However a kitten can disrupt a household and it is sometimes easier to take on a grown cat.*

Above: *Cats and dogs usually make good companions. Here the kitten is more wary than the pup and has fluffed up his fur so as to look as formidable as possible.*

kitten, a young adult, or an older cat? Male or female? Mongrel or pedigree – and if pedigree, what breed? 'All cats,' the old adage has it, 'are grey in the dark,' and the basic character of the cat will be much the same whatever its parentage, colour or pattern or length of coat, but there is a bewildering variety from which to choose.

The main differences between the different breeds of cat are in pattern and colour, coat length and overall body conformation and many people will be influenced solely by the cat's appearance, responding to the lithe Siamese, the cobby short-hair or the luxuriant long-hair according to their taste. Certain breeds have gained a reputation for having particular characteristics, and these are discussed in the next chapter, but a cat's personality does not necessarily conform to its colour and type. I have known long-hairs as neurotic as the most highly-strung Oriental, and Siamese as soft-natured as a silk-cushioned Persian.

One factor which you must take into consideration is the length of the coat: long-haired cats require daily grooming, and if this is neglected you may have to give up even more of your time to removing matts and tangles from the fur.

Most people automatically think of having a kitten when they decide to acquire a cat, but there are occasions when an older animal would be better. If you take over a cat you know, you will have some idea of its character and temperament and its general health record. You will not have to train it and there will not be the problem of a small animal always under your feet. For older people, caring for a young kitten may be a strain, and an older cat will be quieter and more settled in its behaviour. However, it is not particularly easy to train an older cat out of bad habits: the patience this requires will be just

as great as that needed to overlook a young kitten's misdemeanours.

Should you choose a male or female? Unless you intend to breed from your cat, it does not really matter, as you should have the kitten neutered. Too many unwanted kittens are born and you should not be responsible for increasing their number. Neutering will make life more comfortable, for it will remove the urge to spray from toms and end the sometimes difficult problem of controlling a queen in season.

Many people never really 'choose' a cat: they take in a stray or are themselves 'chosen' by a cat who moves in on them. My first cat was a tiny coal-black kitten, barely weaned, which appeared from a bomb-wrecked building during a World War II blitz and followed one of my aunts home. My grandfather took it in, fed it and made it a comfortable place to sleep. Overnight it wrought havoc in his house as it explored and amused itself, tearing up a newspaper and attacking his spectacles which, in the morning, lay shattered on the floor!

He brought it to my home tucked inside his jacket (on the rattling, clanking tram-ride it had wriggled into his sleeve), perhaps the nicest present I have ever received.

If you take in a stray you should always try to find its original owners if possible, for they may be worried sick at losing it. If it wears a collar with an identification disc bearing their address or telephone number you will have no difficulty in tracing them, but if it does not have a disc check with local police and veterinary practices to see if they know of a missing cat that fits its description. Ask a local shopkeeper to put a notice in the window and ask neighbours if they know of anyone whose cat is missing. Only when you feel quite sure that the original owner cannot be traced should you begin to consider the visitor as your pet. Since you know nothing about it you should take it to a vet to make sure that it is healthy, and if you already have a cat you should keep them apart in case it is suffering from some sickness which could be passed on.

If you cannot trace the owner, and neither want to keep a stray yourself nor know of anyone else who does, consult the local animal welfare organizations to see if they can find it a home, although, sadly, far too many unwanted cats have to be painlessly destroyed. You may be offered a kitten by friends or neighbours whose cat has had a litter. If they know who the father was you may be able to get some idea of what the kittens will be like when adult, and knowing the mother's home and her personality will give you some idea of their potential character.

Do not be pressured into giving a cat a home. If you are not fully prepared to give it the care and attention that it will need throughout its life you should not undertake the responsibility. Food, cat-litter, veterinary bills, boarding catteries and other expenses may not be individually large but over a cat's lifetime they can add up to a sizeable amount. You must find the time to make sure the cat is properly looked after, and be prepared for the inroads that its care will make upon your own life, which may not be very great but will be a small restriction upon your own freedom. Your action involves the life and happiness of a feeling, living creature: you must not follow a sudden whim, respond to the instant attraction of an appealing kitten or be talked into adopting a cat without thinking very seriously about the responsibility of ownership and all that it entails.

The animal shelters run by the animal welfare organizations are another source from which you might choose a cat, especially if you have no predetermined idea of what type you want, and there will be the pleasure of knowing that you will probably be saving its life. Most abandoned cats in welfare shelters will be mongrels, but you may find one of pedigree breed, although almost certainly without the documentation to prove its breeding.

Left: *When deciding on what type of cat to have remember that long-haired cats, whether mongrel or pedigree, like these Cream Longhairs, need a great deal of grooming and you must find time to brush them every day.*

Above right: *This tortoiseshell and white queen guards her feeding kittens jealously.*

Four-point landing

Cats seem to be able to leap from considerable heights and land quite safely. With their backs arched and all four legs extended they cushion their fall and absorb the shock without serious injury. However, if they are not wide awake or fall with the body vertical they cannot adjust themselves to make a proper landing, and from a great height the impact could be great enough to injure their legs or crack their jaw if it strikes the ground.

Young kittens, especially, may run up a tree or climb up to a high shelf indoors and then begin to panic about getting down again. Frequently, just as they are about to be rescued they will pluck up the courage to leap down.

The cat's ability to twist its body and orient itself to make a level landing used to be thought dependent upon the sophisticated structure of the cat's inner ear which gives it such a good sense of balance, a factor which also seems to protect cats from seasickness or the effects of the movement of a car which afflict so many dogs and humans. Experiments conducted by British scientist Donald Macdonald with a 15-year-old cat deaf from birth suggest that this is not the only contributing factor. Letting the cat fall from comparatively low heights onto a rubber mattress, which ensured that no injury would result, he found this cat perfectly able to right itself, yet when it was blindfolded it was not only unable to correct its position during the fall but was very slow to right itself after it had landed. Since the cat had been deaf from birth it cannot have been using experience gained in youth, and retained when hearing was lost, and it must have been dependent upon vision. Sight seems to register the relationship to the horizon, while parts of the ear probably sense the position of the head and any rotation, although this function can be confused by rotating the cat before allowing it to fall.

Shelters usually make a small charge or expect a donation towards their costs. Choose a fit and healthy animal, and resist the natural urge to succour the sickly-looking waif, as the chances are that many of the shelter cats will not find owners, and it is better that those that do are the ones with the best chance of a healthy and trouble-free life.

Pet shops are an obvious place to look for a new pet. Many are good and well run, but some are not. Some keep animals on the premises, others may be able to obtain a cat for you or put you in touch with a breeder for whom they act as agent. If you are looking for a mongrel you may well find what you want, but the same advice applies as with cat shelters: do not let your heart be melted by a pitiful waif. In fact, if you see any indication of sickness or disease you would be wise to avoid buying a cat from that shop until you are quite certain that any risk of continuing infection is well past.

For a pedigree animal you will usually do better to go directly to a breeder. The strongest and best-looking kittens will almost certainly be the first to be sold directly from the cattery and only those left over find their way into the pet shops, unless the cattery is very remote or the owner prefers not to handle sales directly with the public. For the kitten there will be less disruption to its young life if it goes directly from its mother to its new home.

Before buying a pedigree animal, and especially if you intend to breed or to show your cat, go along to a few cat shows; this will give you a chance to compare cats of the breed, to make contact with breeders and gain expert advice. You may even see a breed you did not know and change your mind entirely! You will also be able to contact breeders through advertisements in your local press and in the journal *Fur and Feather*, which publishes news about the cat world in Britain. Veterinary practices

will probably also be able to put you in touch with local breeders, and the Secretary to the Governing Council of the Cat Fancy will be able to supply lists of breed clubs and of shows.

A breeder may not have a kitten available just when you want one. Plan ahead. A visit to a breeder's will enable you to assess the quality of the strain, to see whether the place is well run and the other cats are healthy, to get an idea of the personality the kittens may have and to find out more about the breed and the care that the cat will need. You can put your name down for a kitten as soon as one becomes available. Try to see the

Above: *When choosing a kitten for a pet, look for indications of good health. Beware of those with dirty ears, runny eyes or nose, too rounded a belly which might mean worms, or signs of diarrhoea. All these indicate parasites or infections.*

Right: *Like the kittens above, this young cat would make an ideal pet. It is displaying an inquisitiveness which is both natural and healthy.*

litter of kittens with their mother. This will be an extra way of checking their age and health. Watch the kittens at play and you will easily see which are the strongest and most lively. Avoid any kitten with runny eyes, blocked nose or dirty ears. Make sure the rear end shows no sign of diarrhoea. Such signs would discourage me from buying from that breeder at all, unless I knew the establishment well and could be sure that this was an isolated case of sickness. You have the right to insist that the breeder has the kitten you choose inspected by a veterinarian and supplied with a certificate of its soundness and fitness.

Any sensible cat person will advise you to choose the strongest and fittest kitten: do not let your sympathies be drawn by the runt of a litter, even if it does seem to have the most engaging personality. However, one of my present cats was the runt, and probably only survived because it was hand-reared by the breeder, but it has certainly not grown up a weakling. Nevertheless, unless you are prepared to spend time and trouble in caring for it and paying veterinary bills, you must be strong-minded. I do not suggest that you should never buy the last kitten left in a litter, for all should be fit and healthy, and sometimes a breeder with just one kitten left will let it go at a lower price to make the cattery easier to run. Do not look for bargains, though, for that way you may end up encouraging unscrupulous

back-street breeders. Cat breeders are almost all amateurs and not in it for the profit. If you ever rear a litter you will realize how comparatively reasonable most of their prices are.

Assuming that none of a litter have the tell-tale signs of neglect or disease, rickety legs or other faults, but are a picture of glossy-coated, bright-eyed health, how *do* you choose which kitten? You probably will have no trouble at all, for one of them will decide that it likes you and will pre-empt your decision. You may find that two kittens in a litter always play with each other: if you can afford to feed an extra mouth, and particularly if you will be keeping your pets indoors and you are out for most of the day, why not consider having both? They will be playmates for each other when you have to leave them.

A kitten should stay with its mother until it is at least seven weeks old; it must be fully weaned and able to fend for itself before it goes to its new home. Some breeders insist on keeping them longer, despite the added cost to themselves. Never ask if you may take a younger kitten away, even if it seems independent and has formed a clear attachment to you.

A kitten of eight to ten weeks of age still has plenty of growing up for you to enjoy and will adapt easily to the ways of the household. It will also have learned some basic life skills such as stalking and fighting from its mother and during the time spent playing with its siblings.

When collecting the kitten you should be given a certificate to show which inoculations it has had and a note of when booster injections will be required. If no inoculations have been given, a visit to the vet to have them done should be rapidly arranged. With a pedigree cat you should also receive a copy of its pedigree, and, if there is any possibility of you wanting to show or breed the cat, you will also need its registration certificate and certificate of change of ownership. Registration formalities do not have to be completed before you take the cat, but should be completed as soon as possible. Many breeders will also give you a diet sheet, or at least information on the cat's former diet. Keep the cat on the same food at first – it is having to adjust to quite enough changes in moving home and losing its mother's care – and do not introduce a different diet until it has settled in.

Do not try to bring the cat home in

Below left: *A travelling basket is essential equipment for collecting your cat, taking it to the vet and for any journey. One that opens at the top makes it easier to lift an uncooperative cat in and out as required.*

Below: *A bed of their own will please many cats. They like the privacy which it gives them.*

Right: *Young kittens can often be accomplished climbers but keep an eye on them as they go exploring in case they get into difficulties.*

your arms or tucked inside your coat, but get a proper travelling basket. It is always safer for the cat to be in a basket when travelling, even in a car, for a sudden noise or distraction may intrigue or startle it into darting off or getting in the driver's way, and a young kitten will be especially frightened and wary. The basket will give it a small area in which it can feel secure and on a long journey, once it has got over the initial excitement, it will probably settle down to sleep. If it is agitated and anxious, talk to it and reassure it. If it is a 'cage' type basket or has a barred panel you can fondle it gently through the bars – but not if you are driving! I often travel with a cat, even with one that has not been lead-trained, wearing a collar and lead so that I can let it out of the basket to sit on my lap or on the seat beside me: but it is essential to keep the lead short and the cat close so that it cannot jump down and scuttle beneath the seat or try to explore a railway carriage; and I would not recommend this to anyone who is not very well used to cats and their ways. A confident cat will enjoy watching the world go by and the interest it arouses in other passengers but, especially if it is not immunized or has only recently been done, do not allow it to risk contact with other animals or people.

Plan to collect a new cat and take it home at a time when you will be able to give it plenty of attention and there will not be a lot of people about or activity which might frighten it. Do not choose a day when you are going to have to leave it for long periods. The very worst time would be in the middle of a children's party: an animal needs gently to explore and reassure itself of the safety of its new surroundings, and would be frightened by the excited attention of a roomful of children.

A kitten makes a delightful present for a child but the giver should be certain first that both child and parents really do want to have a cat and are prepared for the care it needs and the responsibilities it brings. If the gift is for a birthday, Christmas or some other festive occasion, the day itself will offer quite enough excitements and distractions without the cat's arrival. Perhaps part of the celebration could be the present of a travelling basket or a visit to the breeder to choose the pet, which can be collected later when things at home are more tranquil.

Introducing the breeds

Dogs have been bred selectively for centuries, sometimes, perhaps, solely for their looks but in the main for their working suitabilities: the different breeds are physically adapted for particular jobs, and their personalities reflect their working roles. Perhaps, in the breeding of cats, the kittens of a particularly good mouser may have been considered more desirable than those of a less able cat. In the past certain unusual and imported types attracted fashionable interest and high prices but not until the nineteenth century, about the time when the first cat shows were held, does there seem to have been any serious attempt to plan and control breeding. Even then it was done only for physical appearance.

Left: This charming, wide-eyed kitten is a Seal Point Siamese, which is one of the most popular breeds.

Below: A Brown Tabby Shorthair and a Tortoiseshell and White Shorthair differ only in their colour and markings.

During the past 100 years many different patterns and colours have been developed and fixed by cat breeders, even the most common breeds being refined to conform to strict standards laid down by the world's cat organizations. Between them, the various cat registration bodies now recognize over 100 different breeds of cat. Not all are accepted in every country or by every body, and even quite minor variations of a basic breed may affect its acceptance by a particular society.

Mongrels – 'moggies', alley-cats, whatever you like to call them – are cats of random parentage which do not conform to the breed standards. Their pedigree is unknown, even their paternity may be uncertain, although similarity of appearance between a local tom and kittens in a litter may suggest the father's identity. Even when it is unknown, all cats have a pedigree, but the term 'pedigree' cat is generally taken to mean one which is pure-bred through several

generations, with its ancestors all of a particular breed. In Britain, registration forms for pedigree cats record the colour, names and breed numbers of a cat's parents and grandparents, and by consulting the records for those earlier generations it is possible to trace its ancestry much further back. To those familiar with the reputations of the cats concerned it is possible to see any genetically undesirable or, alternatively, any particularly attractive feature as it appears in the line.

Cats must be registered to compete in most shows and care is taken to see that names are not duplicated, so you may find that the name you have chosen for the cat is not acceptable because it, or one so like it as to be confusing, has already been used. Many breeders register a cattery name, known as a prefix, by which all their cats are known, used before the cat's individual name. This not only immediately identifies their cat's origin but also makes the choice of original names much easier, as no one else may use the cattery's prefix. In the United States suffixes (which follow the name) are also permitted.

Pedigree cats are not necessarily any better than ordinary moggies but they will certainly be more expensive. A mongrel can have just as much personality, intelligence and beauty – perhaps even more – than a pedigree cat, but its offspring will not be so predictable in appearance.

Perhaps because the development of the individual breeds has been in the hands of a relatively small group of breeders, and from a small number of base stocks, some breeds have gained a reputation for particular personality traits. The British Blue, for instance, is said to be highly intelligent and to have a placid and gentle temperament. There is no breed, though, that can be claimed definitively to excel at mousing, retrieving or standing guard in the way that dog breeds have

Left: The Seal Colourpoint was created by breeders who wanted to add the colour and pattern of the Siamese to a typical long-haired cat.

Above right: There are many attractive cats which do not conform to any breed standard. The white chin and chest patch would debar this tabby from the show bench, but its owners probably consider it to be just as beautiful as any cat with an impressive pedigree.

Drop-eared cats

Wild animals almost invariably have pricked-up ears – the elephant is a rare exception. Ears that droop are usually a sign that a species has been domesticated for a very long time, as with the pendulous ears of some dogs.

Cats, which use their sensitive, pricked-up ears to pin-point the source of any sound, could be at a great disadvantage in the wild if their hearing was in any way impaired and if a breeding abnormality did produce drop-ears natural selection would probably operate against the development of a drop-eared strain. Nevertheless, as long ago as 1796 a British magazine asserted that in China 'an empire very anciently policed and where the climate is very mild, domestic cats may be seen with hanging ears'. That report was not authenticated, nor is there scientific evidence to support references to drop-eared cats in early books of natural history, though that is not to say that they did not occur.

At the latter end of the eighteenth century a sailor returned from China with a drop-eared cat which, he claimed, came from a breed that the Chinese reared for food, but it was not until 1938 that zoologists found a second example. This seemed to be a rare mutation which was initially thought to be restricted to white long-haired cats.

In 1961, a mutant cat with ears which folded forward and downward appeared in Scotland. Controlled breeding produced a variety of short-haired cats which retained the characteristic and they were given the name of Scottish Fold. Similar mutants have since occurred in Germany and Belgium and they have also been imported and bred by American breeders.

The Governing Council of the Cat Fancy has refused to recognize the Scottish Fold as a breed in Britain but it was recognized for registration by the American Cat Fanciers' Association in 1974.

become specialized. Such skills may be acquired in play as kittens and reinforced by human encouragement. It is difficult to know whether recurrent skills or temperament in a particular strain are inherited or have developed because they have been brought up by the same breeder or by owners with a similar way of treating them – for cat breeders have not so far selected mates for skills but almost entirely for physical characteristics, with perhaps a little consideration for temperament. I believe that the owner has a great influence in a cat's personality. A cat that is played with when it is a kitten and allowed to join in all kinds of human activity will expect plenty of involvement in its later life. A kitten brought up by a neurotic owner will probably become a neurotic cat. Heredity will play its part but conditioning is also very important.

Domestic cats divide roughly into two main types: long-haired cats and short-haired cats. Shorthairs, in turn, may be rather chunky or have a sleek and elegant oriental look. There are also a few exceptional cats born with almost no hair at all. Pattern and colouring can vary widely but it will be within the colour range of black, white, and red and the weaker forms of these colours, brown, blue and cream or a lilac shade.

The most commonly seen coat among cats is the tabby pattern, a marking which is genetically dominant over other patterns. The name tabby probably comes from Attabiya, an area of the city of Baghdad, which was once famous for a kind of watered silk, or taffeta. Produced by local craftsmen, its pattern is similar to that of the cat's coat.

Two totally different forms of tabby pattern are recognized: the Standard, or blotched, and the Mackerel, or Tiger stripe. The Standard form has three dark stripes running down the spine, a butterfly pattern across the shoulders, whorls on the flanks and two narrow lines across the chest. Legs and tails are regularly ringed and delicate pencilling decorates the face. The Mackerel type has evenly spaced rings running around the body. A variation of the tabby is the spotted pattern which is shared by many wild species of cat. It is surprising that it does not appear more frequently in domestic animals. It is often seen in the eastern Mediterranean, but is less common in Western Europe. It has also been suggested that a further mutation of the tabby produces a grey cat with stripes on face, legs and tail.

Since the stripe is the more frequent natural wild marking it is surprising that the blotched pattern has now become the most common in domestic cats in many parts of the world. It was already common in Europe by the middle of the eighteenth century and, a century later had reached India, although the striped pattern is still as common there. There is an extremely high proportion of blotched cats in London and geneticists believe that changes in pattern and colour take place more rapidly in cities. Dr Neil Todd, an American researcher, believes that it is possible to date the introduction of a cat population to a territory by the frequency of occurrence of various coat colours; after being imported by settlers the cats slowed down their rate of change whilst their urbanized European relatives continued to change, producing darker coats.

Surprisingly, it is not black but white which is dominant over all other colours. White is very conspicuous and pure white cats with blue eyes also tend to be deaf, a fact first recorded in 1828. Both these factors would be a disadvantage to a predator and probably account for the failure of white cats to dominate numerically. White spots, however, are frequently seen, especially on the

Right: *A moggie short-haired kitten, with a Tortoiseshell and White and a Brown Tabby in its parentage, has much more interesting things to do than worry about his ancestry!*

Below: *The pale coat of this young Seal Point Siamese will gradually darken as it grows older.*

Indian continent and in Malaysia, where white may have an advantage in reflecting the sun and keeping down body temperature. White blazes on the face and chest are nearly always passed on to offspring.

The restriction of colour to the face, ears, tail and lower part of the legs, as in the Siamese cat, is an imperfect form of albinism which is recessive to solid colours. A characteristic carried by a recessive gene, though passed on to the offspring, remains dormant unless both parents carry that characteristic. A Siamese cat mated with a solid-coloured cat will produce solid-coloured, not Siamese kittens because the solid colours are carried by dominant genes. Albinism is controlled by a different gene from the dominant white.

Patching and mingling of colours, ticking of individual hairs and differences in fur texture all play their part in delineating the different known breeds, and from the basic colours, patterns, coats and conformations, enthusiasts are always trying to create new variations to meet an aesthetic ideal. Such new types are not recognized as a new breed until they have been shown to breed true to type and have gained the acceptance of the registration bodies.

'What do all these differences matter?' you may ask. 'Surely they are all cats?' Certainly the basic feline qualities are more important in a pet than any minor differences of shape, feature or colour. Even among pedigree cats the individual owner or breeder may prefer a slight variation which goes against the official description, and there are many stunning mongrel cats. However, most people, for some strange reason, feel the need to categorize things, to compare and control and to introduce a measure of conformity. Indeed, once a particularly attractive breed has been produced it is worth ensuring that the type is preserved, although changing tastes will produce modifications in what is generally considered ideal.

Short-haired breeds
The British and European standards for short-haired cats require them to have a compact and powerful body with a broad chest, strong, short legs, rounded paws and a shortish tail that is thick at the base and rounded at the tip. The head should be round and broad, with a short, straight nose, firm chin and round-tipped ears set well apart. The neck should be short and thick and the eyes large and round and most commonly orange or copper in colour. The coat should be short and dense.

Most European breeders accept this as their short-hair ideal but in America the various breed and registration organizations, although differing among themselves on what breeds they accept and on minor points concerning some of those they have in common, are agreed in requiring a different conformation (the shape and proportion of the cat's body) for the *American Shorthair*, or *Domestic Shorthair* as they also call it. The American cat is longer in body, leg and tail and is particularly powerfully built. Its large head is set on a slightly longer neck than that of the European cat and its rounded head, slightly longer than it is wide, has a well developed chin, a longer nose and a slight slant to the outer lower edge of the eye.

In the last decade American breeders have also produced what is called the *Exotic Shorthair*. This cat is closer to the European look and was produced by crossing American Shorthairs with long-haired cats.

The *British Blue* is the breed which most often comes closest to the British Cat Fancy's idea of the perfect shorthair. It is not a very common cat today but it is popular on the show bench. The breed differs slightly from other colour varieties in having a

Right: *A British Blue with its copper eyes and plush coat is typical of the ideal sought by British breeders in a short-haired cat.*

Below: *The combination of shape, eye colour and pure black coat seen in this British Shorthair are comparatively rare in domestic pets.*

particularly fine coat with a texture like velvet plush. In France an almost identical cat is known as the *Chartreuse*, because it is said to have been bred by the monks of Chartreux, who, it has been claimed, originally brought the breed from South Africa.

Although you may see many fine brown tabby cats as domestic pets they are comparatively rare at shows for they have not attracted the attention of many breeders. Perhaps this is because it is difficult to breed a cat which looks exactly right – it is doubtful if many of the pets you see would conform to the strict regulation pattern in every detail – and perhaps partly because breed enthusiasts are less interested in a cat which looks so much like its moggie and alley cat relations. *Silver* and *Red Tabbies* are much more popular on the show bench, although high quality Red are somewhat rare. Only these three

colours are recognized for short-haired tabbies in Britain, but in America both *Cream* and *Blue* Tabbies are also recognized breeds. The *Spotted* version of the tabby, with spotted body and tabby type markings on the face, is also recognized in Britain and may be any colour provided that there is good contrast between the spot colour and the ground colour of the coat.

Solid-coloured British Shorthairs may be White, Black or Cream. Whites must be pure white and may have either orange or blue eyes or one of each (odd-eyed). Blue-eyed Whites almost invariably turn out to be deaf but if, as a kitten, they have the smallest patch of dark fur (which disappears in adulthood) this is usually a sign that they have sound hearing.

Black cats are often melanistic, the colour being superimposed over tabby

striping which can be seen as a ghost pattern in kittens just as the leopard's spots are revealed in certain lights on a black panther, which is a melanistic leopard. Self Black is thought to be an extension of melanism and is dominant but few of the many black cats you see as pets would meet the requirements for the Black Shorthair standard as they are usually sleek and have green eyes instead of the solid shape and orange eyes described earlier.

Some organizations, including American ones, recognize a solid-coloured *Red Shorthair*, but the British Cat Fancy does not, largely because it is so difficult to find a Red which does not reveal basic tabby markings. The British, in common with other bodies, do recognize the Cream, a dilute form of Red, although it is difficult to breed and therefore comparatively rare.

Other patterns recognized for the British Shorthair are the *Bi-coloured*, which is patched with evenly distributed areas of white and any of the other solid colours, the *Blue-Cream*, which has a softly-mingled mixture of these two colours, the *Tortoiseshell*, a cat patched with black and red, and the *Tortoiseshell and White*, in which the white must not predominate and which may have hazel eyes as well as the more usual orange or copper. Blue-Creams, Tortoiseshells and Tortoiseshell and Whites (called *Calico* in America) are all difficult to breed because the red (or cream in its dilute form) is sex-linked. Females have 19 pairs of identical chromosomes, males 18, plus another 2 which do not match. Red seems only to be carried by the female genetic coding and the rare red males that are born usually turn out to be infertile. In Britain the colours for Blue-Creams should be mingled and not separately patched as they are in America.

American organizations and some others also recognize short-haired breeds with *Chinchilla, Smoke, Blue Smoke* and *Shaded Silver* coats (colours all explained under Long-haired breeds later in this chapter). American breeders have also developed a cat with a different textured coat, produced by chance mutation in 1966, the *American Wire-hair*. It has stiff, wiry hair on the head, back, sides and hips and along the top of the tail but the coat becomes less coarse on the chin and the underside of the body. It differs from the Domestic Shorthair only in the texture of its fur.

There very nearly was a Chinchilla shorthair among the British breeds but the breeder who developed it envisaged a coat pattern of tipping which could be produced in any colour and this, recognized in Britain in March 1978, is known now as the *British Tipped Shorthair*. It took fourteen years of selective breeding to develop it from Shorthair Silver Tabbies and Longhair Chinchillas. Its undercoat is as white as possible and fur on the back, flanks, head, ears and tail is evenly tipped with colour to give a sparkling effect. The legs can be very slightly shaded with tipping but the chin, stomach, chest and undertail must be as white as possible. All colours are

permissible with the nose leather and paw pads pink or corresponding to the colour of the tipping. Cats with black tipping should have green eyes, others copper or orange.

The remaining variety of British Shorthair can be any colour but is instantly recognized. This is the *Manx*, a tailless cat named after the Isle of Man. There is a variety of stories and legends to explain how this strange cat first came to be there.

The taillessness of the Manx is a malformation and even when two Manx are mated they may produce a litter which includes kittens with tails and kittens with shortened stumps ('stumpies') as well as the true Manx, which should have no vestige of a tail but have a hollow at the end of the backbone. The mutation which causes this condition is a lethal gene which causes a reduction in the length and number of vertebrae and does not only affect the tail. There can be a high mortality rate in the litters of Manx which are bred to Manx through several generations. The malformation is sometimes accompanied by a malfunction of the sphincter muscles in the anus with incontinence problems which could be very inconvenient in a household pet. The lack of a tail does not appear to affect the cat's sense of balance but Manx are rarely first-class climbers. The Manx is also characterized by having hind legs which are longer than those of other shorthairs. They give its back-end a raised appearance and impart an odd bobbing gait, together with a powerful spring which increases the cat's speed.

The Manx fur is also special, having a soft, open texture with a short dense undercoat. Sometimes there is a tuft of fur in a tail position on the rump but provided that this contains no cartilage or bone it is accepted within the breed standard. Manx are usually intelligent cats and have a reputation for being good mousers and adept anglers.

If you want to own a pedigree cat of the British or American short-haired breeds your choice must be largely an aesthetic one. The Manx looks noticeably different and may cause more headaches if the intention is to breed, and the Silver Tabby and the British Blue may possibly have gentler natures than other colours but, colour and pattern apart, the

difference between one individual and another may be more noticeable than that between different breeds, and it is impossible to offer objective advice. Of one thing you can be certain: short-haired cats will definitely be less demanding of their owners' time than long-haired or oriental types. They will require less grooming than the former and, unless brought up to expect it, will not insist on as much attention as the orientals demand.

Foreign Short-haired breeds
The use of the word 'foreign' to describe this group has no connection with their place of origin and the frequent term 'oriental' is also a misnomer, although some types have been introduced from eastern countries and oriental origins are claimed for others. The term is used by the Cat Fancy as a convenient way of distinguishing them from the British and American Short-hairs.

The foreign type has a longer, slimmer body than the British or American Shorthair, with a long tail and slender legs. The head is wedge-shaped, with large pricked ears and slanting eyes.

The best known of this group, and probably the most popular of all breeds today, is the *Siamese*. The breed's distinctive pattern of dark areas, or 'points', on the lower legs, tail, face and ears has appeared occasionally in many countries; it is a dilute form of albinism, but it has been claimed that the first in Britain was brought from Thailand in 1884 and had been given to its owner by the King of Siam. Thai friends tell me that they have never seen a Siamese cat in their homeland but there is an ancient scroll of pictures and verses, dating from about 400 years ago, which describes and shows cats of Siamese type referred to as Vichien Mas. Today, however, there are more such cats found in Europe and America than have ever lived in Thailand.

The first Siamese cats in Britain were much heavier in build and had much rounder heads than the type

Right: *The British Tipped Shorthair is one of the most recent breeds to be recognized by the Governing Council of the Cat Fancy. There are also several other experimental breeds introducing new colours and patterns which currently await recognition.*

which is admired today. They were cream-coloured with very dark brown points – the colour we know as Seal. Later a Blue Point was introduced and now there is a whole range of Siamese colours: Chocolate, Lilac (or Frost, as it is also known in the United States), Red, Tortie, Tabby (in which the tabby-marked points can be any of the first four colours) and Cream. All colours have brilliant blue eyes. The Cream Point has only a provisional standard in Britain and in America the Red, Tortie and Tabby Points are classed separately from the Siamese under the official name Colorpoint Shorthairs. An Albino is also recognized in America. The Siamese, together with the other Foreign Shorthairs, does not require elaborate grooming. A regular brush with a short-bristled brush will remove loose fur and save your furniture from being covered by moulting hairs, and a rub with a chamois leather, or even simple hand-grooming, will help to keep a sheen on the coat. On the other hand this breed will be very demanding of your time and attention. Siamese like to be involved with their owners and can be very jealous if the attention that they consider their due is given elsewhere. They are highly intelligent, enjoy sharing their games and are considered more easy to train to walk on a lead than most other cats. They can be very talkative, and will engage in lengthy conversations in what is often a rather harsh voice. Females in season have a particularly vociferous call, which some people find disturbing. They seem to mature sexually earlier than other breeds and may well begin to utter these strident cries before they are six months old.

If you keep a Siamese you must be prepared to make time to play with it, especially if it is to be confined indoors. This breed does not enjoy leading a solitary life, and if you are away from home for most of the day,

leaving it on its own, you would be well advised to keep two cats.

Two breeds, the *Foreign White* and the *Foreign Lilac* (*Oriental White* and *Lilac* in the United States) are really Siamese without their point markings. The Lilac differs in that its eyes should be green, not blue. The *Havana* is a self-colour version of the Chocolate Siamese which also has green eyes. While, in Britain, it has retained its Siamese characteristics American breeders have developed it away from the original appearance and now demand a less extreme type with oval eyes and rounded ears and a distinct stop, or break, in the profile between the eyes, something that would be a fault in a Siamese cat.

The *Burmese* Cat, now bred in a wide range of colours, was also originally a rich, deep brown. The first in the West was taken to America from Asia in 1930 and turned out to be a Siamese hybrid. It was mated to Siamese to produce the breed which is nevertheless distinctively different; the body is not so long, the face is shorter, blunter and wider at the jaw, the head rounder and its profile has a distinct break above the nose, and the eyes should be golden yellow. In America round eyes and rounded feet are asked for, making the breed even less like the Siamese.

Burmese with blue coats were granted official breed recognition in Britain in 1960 and since then Chocolate (Champagne), Lilac (Platinum), Red, Cream, Tortoiseshell, Blue-Cream, Chocolate Tortie and Lilac Tortie (Lilac Cream) colours have all been developed.

Left: *The copper-coated Red Abyssinian is a more recent breed than the original golden-brown Abyssinian. Strains of both Blue-coated and Cream-coated Abyssinians have also been created. Ideally these cats should have no white markings but the white chin is very common and is not counted as a fault if it does not extend on to the neck.*

Top right: *A Blue Point Siamese.*

Centre right: *A Red Point Siamese.*

Right: *A Lilac Point Siamese.*

All the Siamese cats have eyes of brilliant sapphire blue, but the body colour and nose and paw leather vary according to the colour of the points. Siamese cats are usually born without any points or mask; these only begin to show as they get older.

The *Tonkinese*, a rare variety so far only recognized by one of the American registration associations, was produced by crossing Burmese and Siamese.

The *Abyssinian* Cat has an *agouti* (ticked) coat like that of the African Wild Cat and it has been claimed that the breed had its Western origin in a cat named Zulu brought back from Abyssinia to Britain in 1868. Pictures of the breed published a few years later look little like the cat we know today and, since cats with this kind of marking occur from time to time in ordinary tabby litters, it is much more likely that the modern Abyssinian is the creation of British breeders.

However, it does look very like the type of cat which appears in some ancient Egyptian art, and some owners like to believe that it is a direct descendant of those sacred animals. Although much more solidly built **than** the Siamese and Burmese, it is of decidedly foreign type.

The coat is the Abyssinian's most important distinguishing feature, each hair being doubly or triply ticked with a darker colour. In the ideal form it should carry no bars or dark markings of any kind, although the back of the hind legs are a darker shade overall and there should be a darker tip to the tail. The belly and the inside of the forelegs should be

paler than the rest of the coat. White markings on the face are undesirable but a white patch on the chin is often present and is permitted, provided that it does not extend to the neck. There should be a darker outline around the eyes. The original Abyssinian colour was a rich golden brown ticked with black, and with base hair a ruddy orange or rich apricot. Since 1963 a Red Abyssinian with a lustrous copper-red coat ticked with chocolate has been recognized as a separate breed. A provisional standard has been issued for a Blue Abyssinian, which has a blue-grey coat ticked with a deeper steel blue and with pale cream or oatmeal base

hair, and Cream Abyssinians have also been bred in some areas.

The breed known in America as the *Egyptian Mau* has its origin in cats which came from Cairo in 1953 and represents a conscious attempt by breeders to recreate the spotted cats to be seen in ancient Egyptian paintings. Mau is the onomatopoeic ancient Egyptian word for cat and the breed is recognized in two colour varieties: Silver, with sloe-black markings on a silver ground, and Bronze, dark brown markings on a light bronze ground. British breeders set about creating a similar cat from tabbies of foreign type which were produced during the creation of the Tabby Point Siamese. They have full oriental eyes, although in America the eyes, although oval and slanting, are faulted if they have a fully oriental look. In both types the eyes may be green, yellow or hazel. One of the American registration bodies specifies an Abyssinian type head in its standard. The British have an added refinement in that the markings on the forehead should resemble a scarab beetle in pattern, recalling the recurring symbol in ancient Egyptian art. The Mau is now known in Britain as the *Foreign Spotted Cat* and should be of full foreign type.

Another recent American breed, somewhat similar to the Mau, is the *Ocicat*, developed from the crossing of a Chocolate Point Siamese with a half-Siamese, half-Abyssinian cat. It has a spotted coat, with tabby markings on throat, legs and tail, and golden eyes. Two colours have been produced: these are the Dark Chestnut and Light Chestnut.

The *Russian Blue* probably has a longer history in the West than the other breeds of foreign type for it may well be a descendant of the Archangel Cat which Elizabethan seamen and traders brought back to Britain from that Russian port. It was introduced to America at about the turn of the century, but it did not become established there until after World War II. It used to be known in Britain as the *Foreign Blue* and the introduction of Siamese blood led to the issue in 1950 of a standard which required an all-blue Siamese cat. The present standard, dating from 1965, reverts to the original form and requires a more sturdy looking cat than the Siamese, though retaining a long and elegant outline and graceful carriage. The head is a short wedge shape with a flat skull, a shorter nose than the Siamese, a strong chin and prominent whisker pads. The skin on the ears is particularly thin and almost transparent. The Russian Blue's coat is different from that of other breeds. It is double, short, thick and very fine, and stands up like plush. Silver tipping to each hair increases its beautiful sheen. Coat colour should be even throughout, and in Britain a medium blue shade is preferred. Eyes are a vivid green.

The breed has a reputation for gentleness and good temper, although they can be very shy. I knew of one which usually hid from strangers and became quite neurotic when, on moving house, it was asked to share its home with another cat. They have a very quiet voice and are not great conversationalists, but they do become very attached to their

Left: *Burmese cats are more heavily built than the Siamese and also have more rounded heads. This Red still has a trace of tabby markings which have always proved to be extremely difficult to eradicate in red self-coloured cats.*

Right: *The Foreign Spotted Shorthair, or Egyptian Mau as it is still called in America, was created to look like the cats of ancient Egypt. It is certainly a very elegant animal.*

owners. Another blue-coated cat is the *Korat*, a cat which indisputably comes from Thailand, where it is known as the *Si-Sawat*. It is medium-sized, strong and muscular, closer to the ground than the Siamese and with a curve to its back. The face is heart-shaped, with large eyes which appear round when fully open but have an oriental slant when partly closed. The eye colour should be brilliant green in the adult, but kittens and young adults may have yellow or amber eyes, and do not achieve their final colour until they are two years old. Ears are large, with a rounded tip, and are set high on the head, giving a very wide-awake appearance. Even among the people of the Korat Plateau, the homeland from which it takes its name, the Korat cat is rare and highly prized. Males have a reputation for belligerence, and may not tolerate cats outside their immediate family group, but at home they usually have a quiet disposition and will take an intelligent interest in all activities.

The Korat's coat is very close-lying and an even silver-blue all over, the sheen enhanced by silver tipping. It lacks an undercoat and the fur on the spine often parts as the cat moves.

Rex Cats are cats with curly hair. They are a mutant form which has been recorded variously in the West of England, East Berlin and Oregon in America. Most cats have a coat made up of four different kinds of hair; the Rex has only one of these hair types (in the case of the German mutation, two of them). This gives a hair length about half that of normal cats and fur of only about 60 per cent of normal thickness, resulting in a plushy coat which will curl, wave or ripple. Two distinct types are recognized in Britain. The Cornish form, developed from a mutation born in 1950, and the Devon, which appeared 10 years later. Although born of ordinary farm cats, they are a definite foreign-type, but the Devon Rex has very full cheeks, a marked break on the nose, large eyes and huge ears.

Rex Cats may be any colour (except Bi-colour in the Devon) with appropriate coloured eyes. Those known as Si-Rex are not a separate breed but simply Rex cats with the typical Siamese colour restrictions.

The *Japanese Bobtail* does not really fit in either the Foreign or the British/American Shorthair groups of breeds. It is sturdily built and well muscled but comparatively slender. The rear limbs are longer than the front ones, which could give a Manx-like look, but when relaxed the cat usually keeps them bent so that the back is carried level. The tail is particularly short and is carried curved so that it looks even shorter, an actual 10–12·5 cm (4–5 in) giving the appearance of a 5–7·5 cm (2–3 in) tuft. The tail hair is long and grows

out in all directions, increasing the bobtail, rabbity look. The head, which should form a perfectly balanced equilateral triangle with gently curving sides, has high cheek-bones, a long nose, big ears and big oval eyes set on the slant.

This distinctive breed has only recently been introduced to America and is still little known in Europe, but has been known for centuries in Japan and appears in many Japanese paintings and prints. In Tokyo the Gotokuji temple is decorated with row upon row of pictures of a cat called *Maneki-Neko*, which guarded the temple manuscripts and, by waylaying travellers and encouraging them to visit the temple, brought it offerings which made it rich. Each picture shows a cat with its paw raised in a gesture of greeting which has become a symbol of good luck. Red, black and white cats are permitted, whether the coat is self-coloured, bi-coloured or tortoiseshell with clear patching, but Siamese points or *agouti* coats are not permitted. The fur is soft and silky and it is claimed by some people that it sheds less than other breeds.

How the Manx lost its tail

Where did the Manx come from? It may have been a mutation originating on the Isle of Man but various legends suggest that the first tailless cat there swam ashore from a shipwreck, perhaps off a merchantman from the East or, it has even been suggested, a vessel of the Spanish Armada.

Some explanations for the Manx having no tail hark back to the Ark. Late to come when called (no doubt it did not like to go out in the rain) the cat was last aboard and Noah was in such a hurry to shut the door and keep out the flood that its tail was cut off by the door. Another version says that while in the Ark the dog began to chase the cat and although she did finally escape, it was at the sacrifice of her tail, which the dog had managed to catch and hold fast in his clenched jaws.

A local legend tells how the native warriors of the Isle of Man, in imitation of the plumes worn in their helmets by some Irish raiders, took to killing cats to use their bushy tails to decorate their own helmets. One old female, determined to save her kittens from slaughter, went away to the top of Snaefell, the island's mountain, to have her next litter. As soon as they were born she neatly bit off their tails and so ensured their survival. As the kittens grew older she told them what to do when they in turn had kittens and so for many generations mother cats bit off their kittens' tails until the time came when they were born without any.

Long-haired breeds

In nature there are no long-haired cats, although several grow ruffs or manes of longer fur. Even the fur of the Snow Leopard and the Amur Tiger, which live through particularly harsh winters near the snow line, grows only to about 12·5 cm (5 in) at its longest which, size for size, would be quite short on a domestic cat. Long hair, which can easily become entangled and matted, pick up burrs, harbour parasites and is very difficult to groom, would be a positive disadvantage to the active wild cat. If spontaneous mutations for longer fur occur it is unlikely that they become established. It seems probable that long-haired strains did not come into existence until the species was already protected by a degree of domestication. It is possible that some human selection was involved in establishing the type.

Historical records do not mention long-haired cats until long after the cat had become domesticated. It has been claimed that a French scientist and traveller, Nicholas Fabri de Peiresc, brought a long-haired cat back from Turkey towards the end of the sixteenth century, and this time coincides with the first reports of long-haired cats in France and Italy.

The first clearly described long-haired cats were given the name *Angora* Cats, named after what is now called Ankara, capital of Turkey. They appear to have been known there for centuries, although they have only been preserved from extinction in recent years by a deliberate breeding programme at Ankara Zoo. Another long-haired cat was described as coming from the Persian province of Chorazan, and was said to have been taken into

India by traders from Portugal. By the time cat shows came to be held in the nineteenth century, both types were known in Europe, but fanciers seem to have preferred the Persian type and the Angora Cat disappeared from the show bench and the home.

For most people the name *Persian* became synonymous with long-haired cats and, although the British Cat Fancy now officially uses the designation *Long-haired*, it is still the name used in many places for all cats of this type.

In recent years the original Angora Cat has been established as a new breed in America from imported cats which were bred at Ankara Zoo and, although not yet recognized in Britain as an official breed, perhaps this beautiful cat will become re-established in Europe too.

The Angora is a small- to medium-sized cat, quite different in shape from the official descriptions of either conventional long- or short-haired cats. Its body, fine-boned legs and tapering tail are all longer than those of the Persian. Its head is small, has pointed ears, a longer nose and tapers towards the chin. It is a lithe and lively-looking cat with a coat of soft, fine hair like that of the Angora goat from the same region (which produces mohair) and the Angora Rabbit, so named because of the similarity of its fur.

The British Cat Fancy may, sadly, lack an Angora breed, but they do have another cat from Turkey. This is the *Turkish* Cat, as it is now officially known, although it used to be called the *Van* Cat, after the area of Turkey from which it comes, a region near Lake Van, where the breed has been prized for centuries. Its physique is like that of the Angora but the difference

in coat gives it a more solid appearance. Turkish Cats have no woolly undercoat and so are easier to groom than Persian longhairs. Most of the coat is white, with auburn markings on the face and tail. Almost any cat discovers that it can swim if it has to, but Turkish Cats seem to take actual pleasure in doing so and also enjoy being bathed, provided that the water is maintained at about their own blood temperature (101°F/38°C). On a very hot day they can be allowed to dry off in the sun, after being mopped with a towel, but otherwise they should be towelled briskly and then brushed dry.

The basic *Longhair* (Persian) type is a much more stocky cat, closer to the standard British Shorthair body shape than to the Angora. The body should be massive and cobby (long and low-lying) and set upon short, thick legs. The head should be round and broad, with full cheeks, a short, almost snub, nose and should show a distinct break (or 'stop') between nose and skull. The ears should be small, neat and spaced well apart; the eyes

Left: *While this ordinary moggy cat's type and colouring will not put him in the aristocratic line-up on the show bench, the soft shiny coat, clear bright eyes and clean ears are all indications of a healthy and well cared for cat.*

Below: *Turkish Van cats love water, hence their nickname 'swimming cats'. When Van Alanya, the world's first champion Turkish cat, became ill, she ran a very high temperature which failed to respond to the prescribed course of antibiotic treatment. After ten days, Van Alanya decided to try her own remedy. This involved sitting in a bowl of cool water – a procedure she repeated three times, and as a result of which her temperature returned to normal.*

round and large; the tail short and thick. In addition to long silky hair throughout the coat, which should have no trace of woolliness, there should be even longer hair framing the head, making a band of fur which can be brushed up into a ruff, and continuing in a deep frill between the legs. The tail should be full with a bushy tip and there should be tufts of hair on the ears.

The long-haired breeds are officially recognized in a wider colour range than that which is accepted for British short-haired cats. Most should have copper or orange eyes, but there are one or two exceptions and, of course, all kittens are born with blue eyes. Both Standard and Mackerel tabby patterns are recognized through the colour range of *Brown*, *Silver* and *Red*.

The Silver Tabby has green or hazel eyes instead of the usual orange and, in this type particularly, kittens are often born almost black, with markings only on the legs and sides, and these often develop into the finest-patterned cats. The long coat makes it difficult to get a clear tabby pattern, but probably helps in achieving a satisfactory Red Self, although in almost every case some tabby markings persist.

In addition to the Red Self, solid-colour long-hairs are recognized in *Black*, *Blue*, *Cream* and *White* (the White being either orange- blue- or odd-eyed) and there are *Blue-Cream*, *Bi-coloured*, *Tortoiseshell*, and *Tortoiseshell and White* varieties, just as in the short-haired breeds.

In Longhairs the British join other registration bodies in recognizing the

Smoke and related breeds. The Smoke, has black feet and face, and black fur along the spine, shading to silver on the sides, flank and mask. It also displays a silky silver ruff and ear tufts. A shimmering effect is created by black tipping of the hairs over a pure white undercoat which shows through when the cat is moving. Often there are three colour strengths on a single hair. The Blue Smoke is recognized on both sides of the Atlantic. The British Cat Fancy also recognizes the *Long-hair Chinchilla*, which is usually smaller than other longhairs, with finer bones and a more dainty look, a difference which goes against it in America where it is expected to be as heavily built as the other Persians.

The origins of the Chinchilla and Smoke types are rather obscure: each has been suggested as responsible for the creation of the other. The Chinchilla also has a pure white undercoat, and the top-coat fur on its upper parts and tail is tipped with black, giving the shimmering silver look. The Chinchilla's eyes are emerald or blue-green and the edge of skin around them is dark, looking like a carefully drawn frame of black. This adds even more to their attractive appearance.

A darker version of the Chinchilla used to be seen in Britain but was dropped from the list of official breeds at the beginning of this century because judges found it too difficult to differentiate between the two types (Chinchillas were probably generally darker then). Some organizations also recognize a Masked Silver Persian, which is like the Chinchilla with a dark-coloured face and dark paws. A blue version of the Chinchilla has also been bred.

American breeders have produced a range of tipped-coat cats in the red colour range which are called *Cameos*. They have been bred in Britain but have not yet been accorded breed status here. Like the Chinchilla and the Smokes they have tipped top fur and a pale undercoat, which can be ivory, light cream or white. The lightest of this group is the Shell Cameo (which may have cream tipping instead of red), then comes the Shaded Cameo, with ticking of a darker red, and darkest is the Smoke Cameo (or Red Smoke as it is also called) which, except for its white ruff and ear tufts, gives the impression of a red-coated cat until it moves and the glittering undercoat shows through. Tortoiseshell and tabby versions of the Cameo have also been recognized by some American associations. All these Cameo cats should have deep copper eyes.

Left: Silver Tabby Longhairs are reputed to be particularly gentle. Their eyes may be hazel or green, but should not be copper coloured.

Above right: Longhairs do not develop their complete ruff, ear tufts and full-flowing coat until they are mature. This Red Tabby Longhair is still quite young.

Right: The Angora has a neater look than the 'Persian' type longhairs and its fur lies closer to the body. Angoras are not a recognized breed in Britain and only whites are known in America.

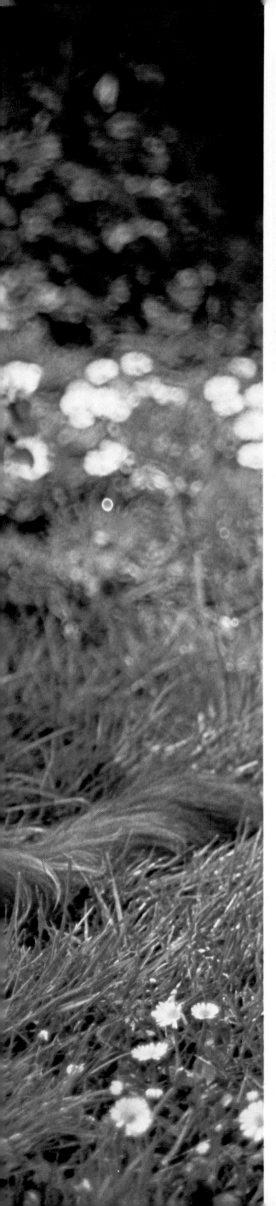

Just as random mutations must have produced the original long-haired cats, individuals with long fur still occasionally occur in the short-haired breeds, and in the 1920s and 1930s attempts were made to develop a long-haired cat that would have the familiar dark points and mask of the Siamese (actually a variation of the albino gene, sometimes called the Himalayan factor). While long hair was achieved by these experiments there was little success in transferring the points pattern to cats which retained the Persian body type. In fact, mating Persians to Siamese usually results in the loss of both features, producing a cat which is short-haired and solid coloured, but the offspring retain the original genetic information and in subsequent matings between them the kittens of the next generation usually include about 1 in 16 with long coats and Siamese markings. Further selection of those closest to a long-hair conformation (the method used by American breeders) or the introduction of other long-hair blood (the method used in Britain) eventually brought success and recognition of a new breed. This was achieved in Britain in 1955, where the name chosen was *Colourpoint* (not to be confused with the American Colorpoints, which in Britain count

Above: *The Chinchilla gets its dazzling appearance from the delicate tipping of its fur with black or silver.*

Left: *The Colourpoint, or Himalayan, has the physique of the usual longhairs with the pattern of the Siamese.*

as Siamese), and two years later in America, where they were called Himalayans. On both sides of the Atlantic the result is a cat with a typical long-hair body, round eyes, long hair, small ears and the characteristic light coat and dark markings of the Siamese.

Seal and Blue Point Colourpoints and Himalayans came first, developed from Black and Blue Longhair stock, and Chocolate, Lilac, Red and Tortiepoint have now been added and all of them have blue eyes. They have retained the soft and gentle qualities of most long-haired cats.

More recent than the Colourpoint or Himalayan is another Siamese-looking long-haired cat, known as the *Balinese*, although the same has nothing to do with its origin. It is in fact a genuine Siamese in every way except that its fur is long. It has the long, lithe body, long legs and tail, wedge-shaped face, almond eyes and large, pointed ears that make the Siamese such an elegant cat.

Specialists in a particular breed are often such purists that they

Griseld and gallipot blew

Roman Mosaics and some medieval manuscripts depict a tabby type of cat, but in England in the early seventeenth century tabbies were fetching high prices (five pounds each) as an unusual form. The contemporary antiquarian John Aubrey, recalled that the 'common English Catt' was formerly 'white with some blewish piedness: sc. a gallipot blew. The race or breed of them are now almost lost'. Gallipot was a kind of turpentine. Edward Topsell, writing his *Historie of Foure-Footed Beasts* a few years earlier, declared that cats were 'of divers colours, but for the most part griseld, like to congealed ice'. These cats sound as though they may have been a blue or silvery grey: grey cats appear in pictures painted by some of the Dutch and Flemish masters, and travellers a century earlier described the cats of Scandinavia as grey. Elizabethan sailors are said to have brought back 'blue' cats from Archangel in Russia. At one time cats with a blue coat were also known as Maltese Cats, although there would appear to be no sound geographical reason why this should have been so.

Topsell also says that Spanish black cats were generally the most highly thought of in Germany and had 'the softest hair fit for garment'.

disapprove of any innovation for fear that it may affect the purity of the breed, and the occurrence of long-haired mutations among Siamese was frequently suppressed. However, two American breeders were attracted by these 'freaks' and found that these long-haired cats bred true. They were recognized as a breed in America in 1963, the name Balinese being chosen for its eastern associations and because Siamese breeders objected to the designation 'Long-haired Siamese'. These lovely animals are now being bred in Britain, too, although they have not yet been accorded official status. Seal, Blue, Lilac and Chocolate Point varieties have all been established.

There is yet another long-haired cat with Siamese colouring which has been in existence much longer than the Colourpoint or the Balinese and was recognized in France in 1925.

Called the *Birman*, it is supposed to have been introduced from Cambodia (then French Indo-China) in 1919 when a pair was given to two soldiers who had aided the priests of a temple during a rebellion. One of the cats died on the journey to Europe but the other, a female, was already pregnant and from her kittens the breed was established in France. Although now known with Blue, Chocolate and Lilac Points (Chocolate and Lilac still awaiting recognition in Britain), the original cats were Seal with a creamy golden coat and dark points.

Below: The Cameo cats are not yet recognized breeds in Britain. The Red Smoke or Smoke Cameo (left) is the darkest form, the Cream Smoke or Shell Cameo (right) the lightest form.

Right: White Longhairs have a tendency to be deaf but if, as kittens, they have the smallest patch of dark fur they will probably be free of this infirmity.

The Birman markings differ from the other similar points in that they have white 'gloves' on their feet, on the rear legs extending over the whole paw and up the back of the hock. This breed is longer-bodied than the usual longhair and has a longer tail, but it is generally shorter in the leg than the Balinese.

An alternative name used for the breed was the *Sacred Cat of Burma* and it has been claimed that cats of this type were kept in Khmer temples long ago, a belief which is confirmed by the story of their appearance in France, but I have never been able to discover whether the legend repeated by many Western cat enthusiasts to explain how they came to get their exclusive colour and pattern is as well known in Khmer culture. This legend tells how a white cat in the Temple of Lao-Tsun, in the time before the Buddha brought his teaching, used to

join with the chief priest in his meditations and in the worship of the goddess Tsun-Kyan-Kse. It was a time of war and the monks had gathered to ask the guidance and protection of the goddess when the chief priest fell dead among them. The cat leapt upon his head and as the priest's spirit left his body the monks saw the fur of the cat change its colour to the gold of the goddess's statue, its eyes to bright sapphire like hers, while its face, ears and legs took on the colour of fertile earth, except for the paws, which were in contact with the old man's silver hair and retained their pure white. The monks watched in amazement as the cat turned its gaze from the goddess to the temple entrance, beyond which invaders could be heard approaching. Recognizing this manifestation of the goddess's power and filled with courage, the monks repelled the attackers and saved their

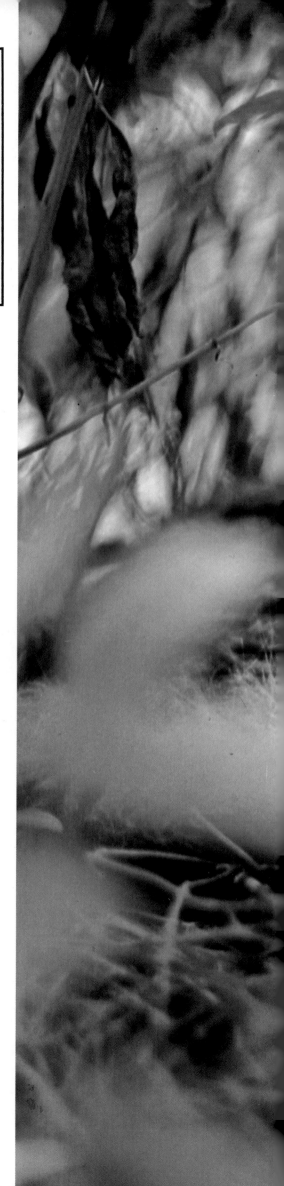

temple. Meanwhile, the cat guarded the body of the old priest, refusing nourishment until, after seven days, it too died, taking the spirit of the priest to heaven with it. From then on all the Sacred Cats took on the colouring of the goddess and when one dies it is believed that it takes a priest's soul to heaven with it.

It is a delightful story, and the Birman is a delighful cat. Less pleasing to many cat lovers is a recent American breed that looks like the Birman but with a heavier body and thicker fur. Known as the *Ragdoll*, it has been developed from a litter of kittens born to a White Persian which had survived a motor accident despite losing the top of her head and one of her eyes. The all-male litter had extremely gentle temperaments and were so physically relaxed that they flopped over one's arm like a bean bag or a rag-doll (hence their name). They showed no fear or awareness of danger and did not appear to feel pain. The implication is that the injury suffered by the mother affected the nature of her offspring as well as producing rather similar (brain damaged?) relaxation in herself. But accidents do not affect genetic structure, so what caused a new mutation affecting an entire litter and subsequent offspring to occur like this?

Their original breeder describes the Ragdoll as 'the closest one can get to a real live baby and have an animal'. They have a tiny voice and are not venturesome but, since their nature makes them an easy prey to other animals and their lack of fear may allow them to lie down in the line of traffic to take a nap, they are strictly indoor cats except for outings on a leash or when being carried. Although Ragdolls are also said to be intelligent and playful, as well as tolerant, they would not seem to be the breed for anyone who likes cats for their feline qualities and there has been criticism of the breed being maintained. A cat which is unable to look after itself demands more than the usual amount of care from its owner.

Less controversial innovations are two long-haired versions of short-haired breeds: the *Somali*, a long-haired Abyssinian, and the *Cymric*, a long-haired Manx. Both of these match their short-haired versions except for the length of coat, and neither of them has received official recognition in Britain.

The Somali, which is not so long-haired as Persian cats, must have full ear tufts, breeches and ruff, although the dense, fine-textured coat may be shorter on the shoulders. The Somali does not need the rigorous grooming which most long-haired cats require, because its silky coat rarely matts.

Aesthetic considerations excepted, grooming is the one feature which sets most long-haired cats apart from the other breeds in choosing a pet. Whatever differences of personality and behaviour there may be between the different breeds (long-haired cats may have a general reputation for being rather placid, but there are very active and playful longhairs, just as there are lazy shorthairs) one thing is unavoidable; if the coat is too long for the cat itself to care for it properly, it must be regularly brushed and combed by the cat's owner.

Right: *This silver-coloured tabby is certainly a very attractive cat in spite of his rather dubious parentage. While the feathered ears, ruff and fluffy tail suggest a longhair the smooth face and shape of the head are those of a typical shorthair but make an extremely good combination.*

Providing for your cat

We choose to keep our pets. They owe us nothing, but we owe them as full and natural a life as we can give them. However, our pets must not rule our lives. They must accept the necessary limitations and discipline to fit into our homes just as we must accept the responsibility of being a pet owner.

A cat needs food, shelter, exercise and good health. In the wild, the business of providing for itself will keep it from being bored, but the house cat, especially if kept entirely indoors, will need activities to keep it lively and interested. As it matures the cat will feel the urge for sexual activity, and to save them from frustration and possible medical problems pet cats should be neutered when young if breeding is not to be permitted. The cat in the wild is a solitary animal and has no need of affection but, for most domestic cats, this seems to be a

Left: A cat will sit motionless for considerable lengths of time.

Below: Even on a winter's day, a cat will try to find a place to catch the sun.

perennial need, perhaps because domestication has psychologically prolonged their kitten stage to stretch through their whole lives.

What equipment should be waiting for your new cat? A sanitary tray (even if the cat is to go outside it is better to keep it indoors until it has settled into its new home), food and water bowls, a sleeping box or basket, a scratching pad or post, brush and comb for grooming, collar and identity disc, cat litter for the tray, and food. Inexpensive plastic litter trays and feeding bowls are readily available and it is scarcely worth improvising with something else. Commercial cat litter is not cheap, especially if bought in small quantities, but is much pleasanter to use than the alternatives. If you keep a small trowel or fork for removing solid lumps you will be able to prolong its use. Cats will not want to use litter which has become very soiled, so frequent replacement will be necessary. Some owners change litter every time it is used (which must cost them a fortune), some only once or

twice a week. I know a cattery which successfully uses only a handful of litter in a tray lined with newspaper which is changed daily. Alternatives to commercial litter (sawdust, sand, torn-up paper or ash) are not so effective as the proprietary clay litters, which absorb both moisture and smell. If you have a ready access to inexpensive peat this could also be used, but put it in the centre of the compost heap so that the heat will kill off any germs with which it becomes contaminated, and after several months, when it is well rotted, you can use it in the garden.

A cat bed can be a specially designed basket with an electric heating element fitted beneath it, a simple cardboard box with torn up newspaper in the bottom and a piece of blanket on top, or anything in between.

A scratching post is needed to protect your furnishings. Cats have to exercise the muscles and tendons which control their claws, and to remove the outer shell of worn claws to reveal the sharp new claw beneath. It is not the scratching that they enjoy but the process, and they like a texture they can get their claws into for the purpose. This will usually turn out to be your favourite carpet or sofa, expensive curtains or fabric wall-coverings. Save them all from destruction by getting a ready-made post or board from a pet shop, or make your own by wrapping a piece of old carpet, sacking or hessian around a stout post or board. It will need to be fixed on a firm base or solid surface. I have made a most effective one by glueing hessian around the cardboard roll on which some fabric had been delivered, and wedging it between the floor and the tread of an open stair. Choose a covering fabric different from any elsewhere in the house if that is possible, so that there is only one place with that texture and nowhere else can be mistaken for a second scratching place.

Even if you are not thinking of letting your cat go out, get a collar, as it is worth trying to teach it to walk on a lead and the collar will hold an identification tag when you take the cat on a journey or to see the vet. Choose a collar with an elasticated section so that if it should get caught on a nail or the twig of a tree the cat will be able to wriggle out and free itself instead of being trapped.

It is also worth making sure that you have some grass growing in the garden or in an indoor pot; cats enjoy eating grass, which helps as roughage and occasionally as an emetic when a cat wants to clear some of the fur it swallows in washing itself.

You will have planned to introduce the cat to its new home at a time when you can give it plenty of attention. Remember that a cat, especially a young kitten which has just been separated from its mother and siblings, must be introduced gradually to its new surroundings. Hopefully, you will already have won its confidence before you get it home. Let it explore in its own time. Open its basket and do not hurry it, let it emerge when it feels confident and

give it plenty of reassurance if it comes to you. Accompany it everywhere but let it decide for itself when a place feels safe or not. Do not allow it to go into places where it will not be allowed to go in future. If later it feels the need to seek them out you can reprimand it or frighten it away, but at this stage do not frighten it or make it feel rejected, simply keep such territory closed off.

If there are already other pets in the house it is probably better to keep them apart at first, but if they encounter each other be very careful. If the newcomer is a young kitten and the established animal an older cat, try the technique used with many animals to get foster mothers to adopt an orphan; transfer the older

54

animal's scent to the newcomer. With a nursing cat, rub a little of its milk on to the kitten, but in most cases the easiest way is to rub a little of the older cat's used litter on to the kitten's fur. For an outdoor cat, a piece of bedding impregnated with the older cat's smell may transfer sufficient scent to prevent antagonism and the kitten may be accepted by the other as some not quite understood extension of itself. It will probably be given a wash and all will be well. Naturally, it is better to carry out this ruse when the established cat is out of the way. I once brought home a new kitten and went to get some litter, leaving the youngster in a basket. It loudly demanded to be let out, bringing the established resident running and trying to attack through the basket's bars. It took over two weeks for the kitten to be accepted and in this case it was the older cat that was more worried, keeping well away from the kitten unless it was accompanied by a human for protection!

An established cat may become very jealous if it sees you lavishing affection on an 'intruder'. Leashing both animals and deliberately

Top left: A litter tray is a primary requirement even if you later intend to let your cat go outdoors at will.

Below left: Cats wash themselves continually, but you will still need to groom them.

Below: A home-made scratching post may help to save your furnishings.

restraining them could make the situation worse. You could play safe and establish the newcomer in a room or area from which you can exclude the other pet or pets. Provide it with a bolt-hole – this could be a cardboard box on its side with only half the lid open – and when the newcomer is feeling secure leave the door or partition open. If the new cat feels threatened when other pets come to investigate, it will still have somewhere to retreat. In most cases, after a little preliminary circling, sniffing and skirmishing, a kitten or other newcomer will behave in a submissive manner to an established cat and will be accepted. It will probably already have recognized the older scent about the house and be aware that it is on another's territory. However submissive a newcomer may be at first that is not necessarily the way the hierarchy will remain. With a dog, in particular, you may well find that the cat soon rules the roost.

From the very beginning, or as soon as possible if you have problems settling in the new cat with other pets, establish where it will be fed and will be able always to find fresh drinking water. Find a place for its bed which is out of draughts (get down to bed level to check for yourself, as there are often gales at ankle height) and not continually disturbed by passers-by. Be accommodating if the cat ignores it, and move the bed to the spot that it has chosen, provided that you do not find it inconvenient. Where a cat should sleep can be a contentious topic – even if you and the cat agree your spouse may not, for one place most cats will make for is your bed!

Whether because it is very attached to you or because that may be the warmest spot in a cold house, many cats, and certainly all but one that I have ever kept, decide that the only place to sleep is on the bed, or even in it! The decision is a personal one, and many people would say cats should be totally excluded from the bedroom. Perhaps a basket in your bedroom might be a good compromise, if the cat agrees to it. At the opposite extreme, some owners still believe that a cat should be put out at night, but to shut a cat out of its home (and it *is* its home too) on a cold wet night seems to me to have neither rhyme nor reason, unless you are a farmer with a rat-infested barn.

Whether you allow your cat to go out on its own or keep it always indoors, or at least under control, will depend entirely upon your own feelings and your neighbourhood. Dangers can exist everywhere: I have known country kittens snatched by a fox just outside a kitchen door, while other cats have lived unscathed to a ripe old age beside a busy main road. Nevertheless, city traffic in a heavily built up area is a strong argument against letting your cat out. Some owners fear theft or poisoning or the risk of infection.

A cat which mixes with others usually builds up resistance to minor ailments, but one kept isolated may succumb to an infection brought in on clothes or a person from outside.

If you live in a block of flats you may not have much choice: internal doors and lifts are not designed for cats to operate and a cat could become trapped for hours if left to wander about unaccompanied. There are attic and penthouse cats with an extensive rooftop territory to call their own. One slip or a thoughtless leap after a pigeon at that height could mean death, although it is fair to say that the risks are probably no greater than on the street below.

Many cats like to climb through an open window and sun themselves upon a window-ledge. If they roll over in their sleep or, half-awake, take a leap at a bird or fluttering leaf they can easily fall, and sustain a serious injury. Cats can jump from considerable heights and land quite safely, but not if they are half-asleep, so either keep the windows shut or fix a protective rail or barrier to prevent them falling off.

Provided that it gets fresh air, a little sunshine and enough exercise, an indoor cat can lead a happy and healthy life, but it will rely on its owner much more. Another cat, or a dog, will be company and make life more interesting for it, but it may not be practical to keep two pets in a small apartment, and you will still need to spend time playing with them.

If a cat is to be allowed outdoors its own door will be an advantage so that it does not have to be let in and out or require an open window which could also provide easy access for a burglar. There is a variety of cat-doors which can be let into a door panel or a hole in the wall. They consist of a flap which the cat can push or lift open, or a circular opening with a flexible seal

which the cat can push through. Choose one which can be locked shut for those occasions when you want to keep the cat indoors. The drawback of a cat-door is that it admits visiting cats if your cat allows it, although some types cannot be opened by an animal unfamiliar with them.

Do not let a cat out of doors until it has become familiar with its new home and feels secure. Indeed, make sure that there are no open windows or chimneys in case it panics if it is suddenly frightened. Let it outside to explore before a mealtime, calling it back in for its food.

Establish regular mealtimes. A small kitten should be fed a small quantity three, four or more times each day; up to the age of three months a kitten's stomach is only the size of a walnut. As it gets older the number of meals can be reduced to morning and evening or even to one daily meal. Personally, I believe two meals a day to be a better arrangement, as the food is not left down on the floor for so long and so has less chance of becoming contaminated.

Cats show decided food preferences and it is impossible to generalize about what they like to eat. At present I have two who will not touch white fish; indeed the only fish they seem to like, and that passionately, are canned sardines in an oil or tomato sauce. One of them is also particularly fond of cooked French beans (and will select them from a dish of mixed vegetables) and asparagus tips, while the other likes to start the day with breakfast cereal (preferably stolen from my dish). One delights in dried cat foods; the other will not touch them but will carry off any bone that it can find. Both devour grass with relish, and without any emetic effect, although they will also eat grass-like leaves from both garden and indoor plants and usually vomit within minutes of swallowing them, although they have no hairballs or other reasons for wanting to regurgitate. I have had cats who would normally eat only one brand of canned cat food, but this has nothing to do with price; one pair favoured the cheapest food

Left: *These Smoke and Chinchilla kittens could not resist the temptation of an inviting ladder!*

Right: *Cats like a high vantage point from which they can survey the world.*

from a well-known multiple store, another a highly advertised and expensive brand.

As a general rule a cat needs about 30 gm of food a day for each kilo of body weight (half an ounce per pound) and rather more if it is a growing kitten or pregnant. The diet should be largely meat with a little cereal and cooked vegetables. Liver will provide some of the necessary vitamins A and E, but large quantities or frequent feeding can cause bowel upsets. Milk will supply both minerals and calcium but too much can cause diarrhoea. Some cats, especially orientals, cannot digest milk when they reach adulthood and they must have adequate calcium in other foods or calcium tablets. Vitamin B can be destroyed by cooking and yeast tablets or extracts make a useful addition which most cats enjoy.

Whether meat and fish is served raw or cooked depends on its freshness and the possibility of it containing parasites. Small and splintery bones should be removed from cooked meat, and sharp and jagged ones from all meat. I also always remove fish bones. Watch out too for bones softened by stewing in which the cat's incisors can sometimes get jammed. Wild cats cope with the bones of their prey, so we might expect domestic cats to be able to manage raw meat, but if in doubt do not take risks: a bone wedged in the throat or piercing the stomach wall is very dangerous.

Exactly what you feed your cat will depend upon price and availability. Most proprietary cat foods are prepared from carefully worked out recipes with ingredients balanced to provide all the cat's basic requirements, and these come in a variety of forms. If you serve dried foods always make sure that there is a bowl of fresh water available: dried food eaten without sufficient liquid can lead to painful urinary conditions. I like to feed my cats on a variety of fresh meats and offals, canned and dried foods. A change of texture and smell adds interest. It is not wise to let a cat become accustomed to only one food which might suddenly be modified by the manufacturers or even withdrawn from the market.

Left: *Cats love to sit in the long grass on a fine summer's day, and this tabby is proving to be no exception.*

I see no reason why cats should not be fed table scraps, provided that they are not given dangerous bones or an excess of very greasy food. I cannot recollect there being any such thing as bought pet foods in my youth. My first cat was fed only on scraps left over from our wartime rations, lights, bones and fishheads begged from fishmonger and butcher, although this caused problems for me: brought up with a waste-not-want-not philosophy, and unused to the size of transatlantic steaks, on my first visit to New York I asked at a restaurant for a doggy bag to take back a piece of fine beef for my host's pet. 'No, no', he said, 'that would never do. If it gets a taste for butcher's meat that animal will never eat what I feed it!' My own cats certainly seem to believe that whatever I am eating must be better than what they are given (even if they have fillet steak and I am eating sausage) and will not touch their own food if they think there is any chance of getting a share of mine.

If a cat refuses a particular meal and you have no reason to think it is sick, do not worry. Do not encourage it to become faddy. It never hurts a healthy cat to go without the occasional meal. As wild predators, cats may have long waits between one successful kill and the next, and their digestive system is designed to cope with successive gorging and fasting. In many zoos the cat family are often given a weekly foodless day as a balancing health measure. If your cat refuses to eat perfectly good food do not spoil it by offering a more expensive treat. If food remains untouched when the next mealtime comes around simply remove the stale meal and replace it with a fresh portion of the same food. Eventually a cat will see sense, although it may make a big display of rejection and bad temper meanwhile. However, be sure that your cat is refusing food out of cussedness and not because of illness before giving it this lesson.

What will happen to your cat if you are away from home? Can you take it with you? Many owners find that if they stay at a week-end home or take their holidays in private accommodation their cat happily transfers to the temporary territory and can safely be let out once it has become familiar with its new surroundings. If the cat is used to regular mealtimes it will return for them – after its last meal before returning home keep it indoors so that there is no sudden panic to find the cat before you go.

Similarly, cats will often happily transfer to a temporary home with others while you are on holiday, but leave them with people the cat already knows and likes and whom you can trust completely. A cat which has to be left on its own for the odd night will not suffer unduly, although it may be rather stand-offish on your return, but for a longer period you must arrange either alternative accommodation or for someone to come in and care for it at home,

providing fresh food and water, changing litter and grooming it as necessary and giving the cat some personal attention. If neither of these solutions is practical it must be found a place at a boarding cattery; during the holiday season it may be difficult to get accommodation and you should book well ahead.

If you do not know a cattery that takes boarders, your vet may be able to recommend one. Inspect it for yourself. Make sure that there is an airy run for every cat, well separated from the next, that there is shelter from the elements and somewhere from which the cat can look out and take the sun if there is any. Assure

yourself that the establishment is hygienic and efficiently run, and if the proprietor does not insist on proof that your cat has an up-to-date immunization against feline enteritis do not use that cattery, for an infection can spread even in the best run establishment. Naturally you will have ensured that your cat is in good health and already immunized, for you would not want to put other cats at risk. Some catteries, at their own discretion, will accept a sick (but not an infectious) cat, especially if it is one that has been coming to them for years. Elderly cats may have chronic conditions which will cause no harm to others but require special attention. It is not wise to put a very elderly or a sick cat into a boarding cattery if it has never been boarded before: the sudden change from its familiar surroundings and friends may be very harmful.

You should always give a cattery the fullest information about a boarding cat, including the name and address of your own vet (even if he is a long distance from the cattery) and details of any recent treatment or known problems. Even though the cattery will have its own vet he may want to ask the advice of the cat's usual vet.

Do not expect your cat to be fed special foods, except for sound medical reasons. Naturally the proprietor will try to follow your wishes and will have a choice of food available in case a particular boarder does not like what is being served at a particular meal, but many cats forget their fads away from home. In the presence of other cats (they may be separated by a wire fence and an alleyway but there is no guarantee that they cannot get through) they may well eat what they are given for fear it gets stolen from them. Fads often disappear during this time, sadly only to reappear when the cat goes home.

If you are taking a cat on a long journey, reduce the risk of toilet problems, by not feeding it for six or eight hours beforehand. If you are travelling with it take some litter along and if it is a *very* long journey provide it with a little food and water.

Left: *Everything becomes a plaything to an inquisitive kitten as it sets about discovering the great wide world.*

Check in advance what arrangements must be made for travelling on public vehicles. Some are not obliged to carry an animal, and bus, railway and airline companies often have their own regulations about containers and documentation. There may also be state or national laws to be complied with, and health certificates may be required. Cats entering Britain, Australia, Hawaii and some other territories must spend time in quarantine on their arrival.

For British owners going abroad on holiday there is no possibility of the cat accompanying them, for it would have to spend six months in quarantine on its return. Indeed, unless they are spending a longer period away and can find no good temporary home where the cat will be happy in Britain, or they are migrating permanently, it would be irresponsible to take the cat with them.

The quarantine regulations protect Britain from the scourge of rabies; as with Australia and Hawaii, Britain's policy is to keep rabies out rather than protect animals against it. This is only practical for island states with no land frontiers. In the United States, subject to veterinary advice which will vary according to the inherent risk in a particular area, cats may be vaccinated against rabies. In Britain this is not allowed (nor in East Germany either, although it is difficult to conceive how the German frontier can be protected from wild animals crossing and introducing infection). Where vaccination is permitted it is much more difficult to trace imported infection and it may also produce an irresponsible attitude among travellers. Even now there are people who try to smuggle their pets into Britain. They are not only breaking the law and risking heavy punishment but, if they are found out, the court may order their cats to be destroyed. Although they would claim, presumably, that they are breaking the law for love of the animal, they are in fact putting at risk not only its life, but also that of all wild and domestic mammals, and human beings in Britain. Rabies can be carried by animals that do not show symptoms of it. It may not strike often, but it is too terrible a disease for any risks to be taken at all.

Cat anglers

He was a very large, handsome, finely marked tabby, with a thick coat, and always appeared very well nourished but never wanted to be fed. He was a nice-tempered, friendly animal, and whenever he came in he appeared pleased at seeing the inmates of the house, and would go from one to another, rubbing his sides against their legs and purring aloud with satisfaction. Then they would give him food, and he would take a morsel or two or, lap up as much milk as would fill a teaspoon and leave the rest. He was not hungry. . . .

. . . The only thing they discovered about his outdoor life by watching him was that he had the habit of going to the railway track . . . and would seat himself on one of the rails and remain for a long time gazing fixedly before him as if he found it a pleasure to keep his eyes on the long flittering metal line.

At the back of the cottage there was a piece of waste ground extending to the river, with a small, old ruinous barn standing on it a few yards from the bank. Between the barn and the stream the ground was overgrown with rank weeds, and here one day Caleb came by chance upon his cat eating something among the weeds – a good-sized, fresh-caught trout! On examining the ground he found it littered with heads, fins and portions of the backbones of the trout their cat had been feeding on every day since they had been in possession of him. They did not destroy their favourite, nor tell anyone of their discovery, but they watched him and found that it was his habit to bring a trout every day to that spot, but how he caught his fish was never known.

Extract from
A Shepherd's Life by W. H. Hudson

Mr Leonard, a very intelligent friend of mine, saw a cat catch a trout, by darting upon it in a deep clear water, at the mill at Weaford, near Lichfield. The cat belonged to Mr Standley, who had often seen her catch fish in the same manner in summer, when the mill-pool was drawn so low that the fish could be seen. I have heard of other cats taking fish in shallow water, as they stood on the bank. This seems to be a natural method of taking their prey, usually lost by domestication, though they all retain a strong relish for fish.

Charles Darwin

In the Battery at Devil's Point, one of the Plymouth defence works, there lives a cat who has a very clever way of catching fish. Fishing has become a habit with her and every day she plunges into the sea, catches a fish and carries it in her mouth into the Naval Guard-room, where she puts it down. The cat who is now seven years old has always been a good mouser and no doubt her experience in hunting water-rats has taught her to be bold and dive for fish, of which, as is well known, cats are particularly fond. Water has now become as necessary to her as to a Newfoundland dog and every day she goes along the rocky shore, ready at a moment's notice to plunge into the sea to grab her prey.

Extract from *Plymouth Journal*, 1828

Looking after your cat

Caring for a cat requires more than just feeding it and giving it a home. You are responsible for keeping it happy and healthy. A cat may seem quite capable of looking after itself, but you have only to look at the strays which are seen all too frequently in our cities, and compare their condition with a well-cared-for pet to realize what a difference your care can make.

Regular grooming will reduce the incidence of hairballs, remove moulting hair which would otherwise end up over your furniture and carpets and help to keep the skin healthy and parasite-free. Daily grooming is essential for long-haired cats. A brush with nylon bristles set into a rubber pad is recommended for long-haired breeds and a baby brush for short-haired ones. There is a variety of brushes specially produced by cat accessory manufacturers: avoid using brushes with metal bristles (which might scratch the skin). Brush vigorously, as most cats enjoy it and it stimulates the circulation. Long-hairs will also require combing. A metal comb is the easiest type to keep clean and a very fine-toothed comb can

Above: *All cats need daily attention to prevent them forming fur balls.*

Left: *Long-haired cats need longer and more frequent grooming than the shorthair breeds do.*

also be used if flea infestation is suspected. Handle tangles gently and avoid pulling at the skin: regular grooming will prevent them occurring. If you have trouble separating matted fur, try moistening it. This often makes it easier to disentangle. Really bad mats may have to be cut away.

I always start grooming by removing any burrs, then massaging the skin with the tips of the fingers, pressing quite hard, the way a barber gives a friction rub. Cats seem to find this invigorating and it loosens dead hair. With a short-haired cat, hand grooming from head to tail will remove much of the hair so that it collects around the rump. Massage and brush in all directions, not just in the lie of the coat. An old nylon stocking slipped over the brush or a piece of chiffon or chamois leather in the hand can be used to give a final polish, and remove any remaining dust from the coat.

Grooming does not stop at the fur. Ears should be gently wiped clean with a swab of cotton-wool if there is an accumulation of dirt, (but do not poke the swab into the ear) and dirt removed from the corner of the eyes. Indoor cats whose claws are not worn down by hard surfaces may grow their claws over-long and these need trimming. This should be done with clippers, not scissors, and care must be taken not to cut into the quick. Hold the cat's paw in one hand and apply gentle pressure to one 'toe' at a time to extrude the claw, then snip the tip of the claw away well below the pink colouration. Use the grooming session as a regular check on the cat's general well-being. Examine the coat for fleas or other parasites and for any sign of skin problems. Check the condition of the claws and paws and inspect the mouth to see that it is healthy and that there is no serious build-up of tartar on the teeth. Slight encrustation can be removed with the tip of a clean fingernail but if it becomes really hardened on, descaling should be carried out by your vet.

Cats rarely need to be bathed, except when they get covered in some substance that is otherwise impossible to remove or to have a flea shampoo. Be prepared for plenty of resistance, although some cats can be very cooperative once they know they are going to have to put up with it anyway! Part-fill the kitchen sink with luke-warm water: grip the cat by the scruff of the neck and support it beneath the hindquarters and lower it into the water, taking care not to submerge its head; quickly apply the shampoo and then, if you do not have a second sink already filled with rinsing water, hold the cat on the draining board while you change the water. Another method is to put the soap or shampoo inside a small canvas sack, pop in the cat, leaving its head poking out, and submerge the cat up to its neck and lather the sack as though it were a sponge. Then rinse twice. If you are giving a bath for medical purposes follow the instructions or your vet's directions precisely, for in many cases no rinse should be given.

Always avoid the use of any soap or other substance containing carbolic, for this is dangerous to cats. After bathing the cat, wrap it in a towel to soak up as much water as possible,

Above: *Daily wear and a little judicious biting and pulling enables most cats to keep their claws in trim.*

Right: *Aerosol flea treatments are available as well as powders and shampoos, and are easy to use.*

Far right: *It is important to check for ear mites, while checking the coat for fleas.*

then give it a brisk rub with another dry one. Next, settle the cat in a warm place and brush it dry. If you are lucky your cat may tolerate an electric hair dryer – though I warn you that mine have always fled in terror. If a cat becomes contaminated with paint or some similar substance, do not use turpentine or other solvents to remove it, as they are as harmful as the paint. Play safe and take the cat to the vet. Small blobs on the fur can be cut off or even swabbed off with plenty of clean water. They should not be left for the cat to try to lick off.

For ridding cats of fleas, dry treatments are more usual than baths. Constant scratching will be the usual sign that fleas are present, or you may encounter one when grooming. I have been lucky: my cats have only ever had the odd one or two and I have been able to catch them during grooming, but some cats get heavily infested. The fleas' favourite spots are around the head and ears, on the back of the neck, around the root of the tail and on the tail. The usual treatment is to dust with a powder that kills the fleas. The safest kinds are pyrethrum and derris dust, but always make sure that what you buy is really suitable for cats: check carefully that it does not contain DDT or any carbolic substance, as not all labelling can be trusted, and some which state that they are suitable for cats are not. To give the treatment, spread out some newspaper on a table and place the cat in the middle. Put a few pinches of powder on its tail and rub it in. Put some on the head and shoulders (make sure none gets in the eyes, mouth or ears), and gradually work it in towards the cat's middle. Comb and brush out the powder and fleas and as the fleas drop on to the paper, crush them. If the cat is very badly infested you can start the treatment inside a paper bag – leaving the cat's head sticking out, of course!

You probably will not have caught every flea so give a follow-up treatment a week later. There is no point just treating the cat. Fleas and their eggs may be in its bedding, or lodged between floorboards and other inaccessible places. Burn or treat the bedding, and be prepared for a reinfestation when any eggs hatch out. Rapid treatment will eventually win out, which is why you need to look out for fleas when grooming.

Fleas are not the only parasite you may encounter. Country cats, in particular, may pick up sheep or cattle ticks and there are various kinds of mites and lice, most of which can be treated in the same way as fleas. Elderly or very sick cats which have difficulty in keeping themselves clean are occasionally vulnerable to maggots, but this does not occur if they are kept clean and well cared for. Do not try to pull off ticks without first dabbing them with a drop of alcohol or ether, to make them let go, otherwise their heads still stick in the skin and start a sore.

A mite infestation in the ears, recognized by a general dirtiness, a brownish discharge and by the cat scratching its ear and shaking its head, is common, especially in kittens, and needs immediate treatment to prevent serious damage to the ear. A few drops of lotion applied over a period soon clear it up in the early stages, but ask your vet to prescribe the treatment, which must be matched to the animal and the degree of infestation. After the first application you can continue the treatment yourself.

Ringworm is not a worm but a fungal infection which shows as ringlike patches on the skin. It is transmissible to humans, so never delay treatment. Most kinds show up clearly under ultra-violet light by producing a fluorescence.

Internal parasites are another common problem, especially with young kittens. It is routine procedure to worm kittens soon after you get them home. Your vet will give you the right pills to match the kitten's size. Pot-bellies, vomiting, diarrhoea and scurvy skin may all be indications of worms, which can be of several kinds. Roundworms are very small and look like thin pieces of string. Tapeworms are segmented and the

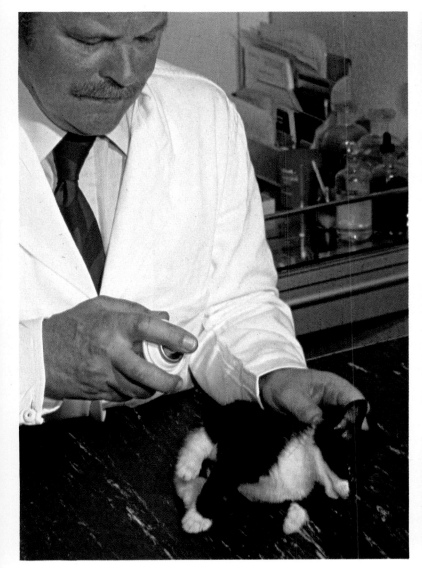

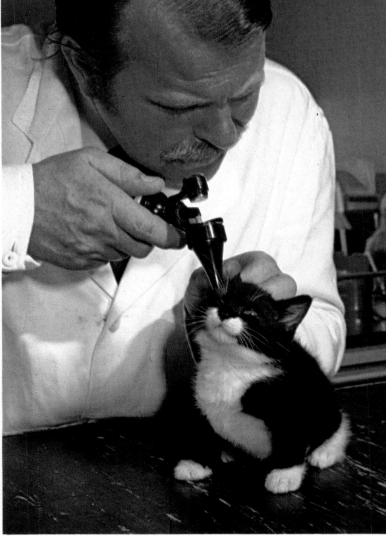

broken segments look like grains of rice, sometimes noticed in the cat's faeces or attached around its anus. If you suspect a worm infection, take the cat and a sample of its faeces (spoon it into a plastic pill box or something similar) to the vet to help confirm his diagnosis.

The most serious of cat diseases apart from rabies is feline infectious enteritis, but fortunately there is a vaccine which offers protection and all cats should be immunized against it, for it is highly contagious and usually fatal. A cat contracting it will probably be unusually quiet and the first obvious symptom will be vomiting, often prolonged and severe, producing froth or fluid stained with bile. There may be diarrhoea, a high temperature and loss of appetite. Although obviously thirsty, the cat rarely drinks but may sit hunched up by its water bowl as it becomes increasingly dehydrated.

Feline viral rhinotracheitis and feline picornavirus infection are two diseases which produce similar symptoms and are commonly known as cat flu. High temperature, sneezing, snuffling and dribbling are typical symptoms. These diseases are not quite as dangerous as feline infectious enteritis but require careful nursing. If a cat survives the first 48 hours it has a good chance of pulling through, but any relaxation of care may lead to a relapse. Forms of peritonitis, leukemia and other cancers, and many other diseases and organic malfunctions affect cats just as they do humans, but this is not the place to give detailed medical advice. If your cat has regular care and attention you will notice those little changes in behaviour as well as the more obvious symptoms that indicate something is wrong. If you have any suspicion that the cat is ill, do not hesitate to consult your vet. He would rather spend time on a needless consultation than be presented with a condition too advanced for proper treatment. Symptoms such as vomiting and diarrhoea may mean no more than a minor stomach upset and going without food for a day could cure the problem, but should they persist or be accompanied by other symptoms do not ignore them.

In treating any sick cat, always carefully follow your vet's instructions, and if they are not absolutely clear ask him or her to explain them again! A sick cat should be allowed peace and quiet and not be continually disturbed by anxious owners, but if it is used to plenty of attention do not ignore it completely. If necessary you must help it perform its toilet and you must see that it is kept clean. Some cats are not very cooperative about taking pills and medicines, but they can be administered quite easily. To give a pill, hold the cat's head in one hand, like a ball, with the forefinger and thumb coming down on either side to the corners of the mouth. Squeeze gently and it will open its mouth. With the other hand hold the lower jaw down with one finger and pop the

Right: *Subcutaneous injections are given into the soft connective tissue between skin and muscle and enter the bloodstream at a steady rate. It is obvious that most cats scarcely feel them.*

Far right: *Two pairs of hands will make it easier to give a pill to a cat.*

Below: *Abyssinian cats make good domestic pets, although they sometimes become attached to one person.*

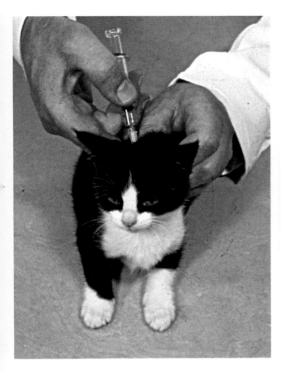

pill on to the back of the tongue. Some people like to use a small spatula or a spoon handle to hold the mouth open if they are afraid of being bitten. Once the pill is in, hold the mouth closed and stroke the front of the throat with a downwards motion until the cat has swallowed. Even when you think it has swallowed, continue a little longer and watch it afterwards, for many cats pretend to swallow a pill but hold it in their mouths and spit it out later!

Medicines are most easily given with a plastic hypodermic syringe without the needle. Your vet will be able to give you one if it is not available elsewhere. It enables the dose to be accurately measured and the medicine can then be squirted between the teeth into the cat's closed mouth, a little at a time. Do not force too much down or it may go the wrong way and choke the cat.

Cats sometimes suffer from an accident or injury. Surface wounds usually heal very rapidly, but should be cleaned and bathed with a weak antiseptic to prevent infection. Sometimes the surface skin heals over an infection, which results in an abscess, especially in the case of bites from other animals. Antibiotics and professional attention may then prove necessary. Serious injuries should be treated by your vet. A cat frightened and in pain may be aggressive, even to its owner, so be careful how you handle an injured animal, and wear gloves when you do so. After an accident a cat may be in shock, and should be kept warm and moved as

---

Cat overboard

It chanced by fortune that the shippes Cat lept into the sea, which being downe, kept her selfe very valiantly above water, notwithstanding the great waves, still swimming, the which the master knowing, he caused the Skiffe with half a dozen men to goe towards her and fetch her againe, when she was almost halfe a mile from the shippe . . .

. . . I hardly believe they would have made such haste and means if one of the company had bene in the like perill. They made the more haste because it was the patron's cat. This I have written onely to note the estimation that cats are in, among the Italians, for generally they esteeme their cattes, as in England we esteeme a good Spaniell.

---

little as possible on its way to the vet.

Many common products in the home are poisonous to cats and should be kept well out of their reach. Disinfectants, weedkillers, paints, petrol and its products can all be harmful. Aspirin is particularly dangerous to cats and must never be given to them. If you know that you have poisons about the house, always try to discover the appropriate antidote. Failing that, if you do think your cat has been poisoned, adminster a 'universal mixture' which a pharmacist will supply for your medicine cupboard or, in a real emergency, make one from one part milk of magnesia, two parts burnt toast (or powdered charcoal if it is available) and one part strong tea (tannic acid). As a last resort, hydrogen peroxide diluted in twelve parts of water will make the cat vomit. However, *never* try to induce vomiting if the cat's mouth has been injured by a caustic substance. In either case get it to a vet as soon as possible.

One of the first things you should have decided before owning a cat is whether you intend to have it neutered or not. To my mind it is

irresponsible to keep an entire tom, except for stud purposes. A tom kept housebound will not only spray your home and make it smell extremely unpleasant, but will also become a very frustrated animal. A tom which is allowed to range free will almost inevitably mate at random and increase the number of unwanted kittens which have to be destroyed. If you do not want to have a litter on your hands an un-neutered female will have to be shut indoors when she is in season and carefully watched to make sure that she finds no way out. Pills which interfere with her natural sexual cycle can be given, but may cause problems if administered for long periods, and failure to mate a female season after season can also lead to neuroses and physical problems. Castration of the male is a very simple operation and spaying (neutering of the female), although much more complicated, is a routine technique in every veterinary surgery. Your vet will have his own idea about the age at which these operations should be performed, and must be consulted when you first have the cat. The operations make little difference

Left: *Cats usually cope with birth quite naturally and easily. The foreground kitten is already a minute or two old. It has been freed from its amniotic sac and the umbilical cord severed. However, its mother has not had time to eat the placenta for she is busy delivering another kitten which she seems to have already freed from the enveloping sac.*

Below far left: *A mother cat will wash her kitten to clean it and dry up the amniotic fluid but even ten minutes after birth it will still look quite damp.*

Below left: *A little while later the white fur of the same Siamese kitten has become quite dry and fluffy.*

Below: *Many cats will try more awkward ways of carrying their kittens before they discover that this is the easiest and most effective way of all!*

to a cat's personality, but they will lose the powerful urge to go hunting for sexual partners, and although a change in hormonal balance may slightly increase the possibility of certain skin problems when the cats grow very old, this is a likely problem with any cat and is much less serious than the injuries which fighting toms frequently sustain or the strain on a female cat of carrying endless litters of kittens, which could also cause you unnecessary problems.

If you are willing to accept the responsibility of kittens – and you should be prepared to keep all of them if you cannot find them good homes – feline motherhood and raising a litter can be an exciting and rewarding experience to share. If you want to control the type or breed of offspring you will have to arrange a mating with a stud cat. Choose a tom whose pedigree and characteristics will balance those of your female, or 'queen' as she would be known in cat-fancy terminology. If there are any faults which you do not want to perpetuate, you can choose a tom in which these features are particularly correct. Breeders offering toms at

stud can be contacted through cat societies and will be happy to advise you on the suitability of the match. You take the queen to the stud when she comes into season, having made preliminary arrangements well in advance. How long she stays with the tom will depend upon the particular stud owner's practice. You will have to pay a stud fee which will include the cost of feeding and looking after your cat.

Gestation in cats lasts about 64 days, and the first sign that a female is pregnant is a slight reddening of the nipples about three weeks after mating. About 10 days later the nipples may begin to swell and you can get your vet to check whether she is carrying kittens. Some queens do not look noticeably pregnant until quite close to the time when the kittens are due. The mother will gradually demand more food and for the last three weeks will probably eat about twice as much as normal. As the demand increases add vitamin and mineral supplements to her diet so that she has enough to form strong and healthy kittens. When the time for the kittens' birth approaches the mother will show signs of wanting to make a nest, and a kittening box should be prepared for her and placed in a warm, dark place, well away from household bustle and lined with newspaper which she will probably tear up. Put her in the box occasionally and if she shows no sign of liking it but tries to make a nest elsewhere move the box there, unless it is totally unsuitable. As the time to give birth approaches you will notice her becoming more affectionate and there may be traces of milk on her nipples and a slight discharge from her vulva, which will become increasingly distended. She may alternate scratching motions with squatting. This is the time to put a warm blanket in the kittening box

and cover it with a clean towel ready for the births.

Some cats like to be left entirely alone when they have their kittens and instinctively know how to deal with everything themselves, others like to have their favourite humans and even other cats with them and may call or fetch you to them when they feel ready to give birth. Some, especially Siamese, may actually delay birth if their owner is not there and try to wait until they return.

Complications are rare in cat births but it is as well to let your vet know when the kittens are expected, in case anything goes wrong. Ask your vet or a breeder to explain exactly the various stages in giving birth, so that you know how to help if

necessary. A heaving of the flanks indicates the beginning of labour, and muscular contractions force the kitten outwards until a discharge of fluid precedes its emergence. It arrives enclosed in a semi-transparent sac which the mother will rip open with her teeth. She will then lick the kitten dry and clear of mucus which might hamper its breathing, sever the umbilical cord and eat the placenta which is expelled after the kitten and which has been nourishing the foetus. Check that a placenta is delivered for every kitten, for if any is retained within the mother it could cause problems. The birth of the first kitten is sometimes a very slow affair and the others follow more rapidly, but there is no regular pattern or timetable and

Cat in the Tower

The young man in this portrait is Henry Wriothesley, the fashionable young Earl of Southampton who was the friend of playwright William Shakespeare and the patron of the company of players to which the poet belonged. At the top right hand corner of the painting is a view of the Tower of London, where the Earl was imprisoned towards the end of Elizabeth I's reign for supporting the rebellion of the Earl of Essex. Near his right hand is a handsome but rather serious black and white cat sitting on the windowsill. The picture was painted during his imprisonment.

The cat was Wriothesley's favourite from his London home, and surprised the Earl one day by suddenly appearing down the chimney of his apartment in the Tower. We do not know how long after his imprisonment the cat arrived, nor how it discovered where its master was. As the Earl often left his palace for his country estates the cat, unless it travelled with him, must have become used to his absences. Why did it decide to look for him? How did it know he was in the Tower? How many chimneys did it try before discovering its master? Or was it pure chance that, on a normal daily outing, the cat made its way past the guards and, climbing over the roofs of the fortress prison, suddenly became aware of its master down below? The questions will remain for ever unanswered, but it is still a remarkable story.

the birth of a litter may vary from less than an hour to as long as six hours.

Soon after the birth the kittens will find their way to their mother's nipples and begin to suckle. Leave them all in peace for an hour or so and then offer the mother some food and milk or water and while she is eating change the soiled towel.

The kittens are born blind, and will not open their eyes until they are about nine days old, but they will already be busy crawling about the nesting box and fighting over nipples, though each may develop a preference for a particular nipple, which saves squabbles at feeding times. At first the mother will wake them up when she wants to feed them. As they get older it will be the kittens who insist on being fed.

The easiest way to sex kittens is to compare them with each other, and, if their mother raises no objections, to do it when they are only a few days old and they have not yet grown much hair. At that stage the anus and the genitals appear in males like two small dots and in females as a dot with a dash below.

When they are a little older it becomes more difficult to distinguish between sexes, although a useful guide will be that the anus and genitals appear much closer together in the female than in the male. Even then, unless you are experienced, you may find, when they are three to four months old and the differences are much more obvious, that you have made a mistake!

They will not see properly until they are about three weeks old (until then they rely largely on their noses) and then they will begin to crawl away from the nest. From four weeks they will start to get their teeth and will probably be showing an interest in their mother's food. At this time offer them a little evaporated milk or thickly-made powered milk and if they lap it try them next with a little cooked baby cereal, then a little very finely minced raw beef and perhaps some lightly scrambled egg.

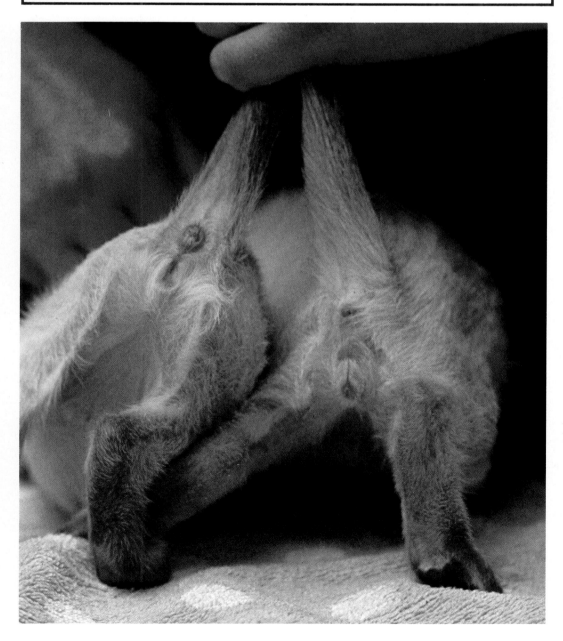

Left: *Sexing kittens is easier if you can compare male and female. The one on the right is male; the one on the left, his sister.*

Right: *These Siamese kittens are old enough to leave their mother and go to their new homes. She will undoubtedly welcome some peace and quiet!*

To begin with the mother's food and litter tray should be within easy reach of the nest but after a while she may prefer to be fed further away, where the kittens cannot pester her or steal her food. For the first few weeks she will clean up all their bodily excretions, but as they start to take solid food she will probably teach them to use the litter tray. If she does not do this you may have to help in their training, and in either case you will have to tolerate a number of 'accidents'.

Kittens should be fully weaned by the time they are six to seven weeks old. Gradually reduce the number of meals (never put down more food at a time than they can easily clear up rapidly or you will find them over-eating and having stomach problems) until they are down to four meals a day by the time they are eight weeks old. The mother may now be showing signs of being bored with them and anyway, they are old enough to go to their new homes.

The animated mousetrap

The cat is one of the most efficiently designed animals in existence which is why the cat family has changed so little in the eight to ten million years of its evolution. You have only to see how smoothly it can move, how powerfully it leaps, how gently it lands and how quickly it reacts, to appreciate how well co-ordinated and sensitive to every stimulus it is.

Cats have a very flexible skeleton of more than 230 bones. Their forelegs can turn in almost any direction, the head can turn through almost 180° and the spine is very mobile, especially the tail. The bones are linked by over 500 strong muscles which are especially strong in the legs and loins, giving a powerful spring, and in the neck and shoulders, which helps them strike down prey. Their brain is highly sophisticated and rather like our own, which is why cats are often used as experimental animals. The part which coordinates movement and controls balance and sense of direction is particularly highly developed, enabling their lithe and agile body to react with great speed

Above: *Although this kitten appears to be in some distress having climbed the tree, he will soon become a finely balanced machine with highly tuned senses.*

Left: *Whilst concentrating directly ahead this tabby walks smoothly on two levels.*

and accuracy. On the other hand the chest cavity is comparatively small, and the cat has a small heart and lungs, so it tires easily. This means that it can have bursts of great activity but they must be interspersed with fairly long periods of rest. The small chest allows more space for the digestive organs which are comparatively large, enabling the cat to alternate gorging on a kill with a period of fasting.

Although consisting of similar components to our own, the cat's legs and arms have different proportions and use. The cat's ankle is the joint half-way up the leg and it walks not on its feet but its toes. Most cats have five toes on each fore-foot and four on each hind foot, but cases of extra toes (polydactylism) are not uncommon. A cat's digits are not developed like human fingers but it uses its front paws with more versatility than is generally realized. It can not only hold things down, it can lift with them, grip things between them, use them to scoop, pat, pummel and punch. The fleshy pads absorb shocks and help to soften any noise, but they are also extremely sensitive. The rear paws are less flexible but are very strong and used in battle. The claws are weapons, help to grip on slippery surfaces or when climbing, and in adult cats can be withdrawn into their sheaths to protect them and to make their footfalls quiet. In kittens and some cats, Siamese in particular, the claws are not fully retractable and on a hard surface they often make a clicking sound as the cat walks along.

The function of the tail is unclear. It is not used for holding on to things as in some species. It seems to play a part in aiding balance, yet the Manx manages without one and cats which lose their tails adapt easily to life.

The cat's fur protects the skin and insulates the cat. In an outdoor animal it becomes thicker as winter approaches, and long-haired cats grow more fur around their haunches. Cats are fastidious about keeping their fur clean and well groomed.

Watch a cat washing and you can see how supple its body is. By bending and twisting it can reach almost every part of its body with its tongue, which it uses as scrubbing brush and comb. The head and neck, which the tongue cannot reach, it cleans by moistening its paws and scrubbing with them.

The rough papillae which cover the tongue and make it such an efficient cleaning instrument, also help to rasp meat off bones but, because they slope backwards, have one disadvantage in that it is difficult for a cat to avoid swallowing anything which becomes lodged upon them. The cat also uses its tongue as a spoon for drinking; and most of the cat's taste-bud cells are on the tongue, although there are others situated elsewhere in the mouth.

Cats are not thought to have a highly developed sense of taste compared with ours, but individual cats most certainly show a preference for certain foods, as any cat owner will know. Smell and texture may play a big part in these preferences but they do not operate alone.

Smell is a strongly developed sense, in which the cats take great pleasure, and in the new-born kitten it is the predominant sense. It is a major means of identification at both long and short range. It is used for location of food, which cats seem unable to see when it is very close, and for tracing potential sexual partners at long distance. Your cat will probably investigate your shopping bag with its nose to see what you have brought home and will sniff you and your clothes to discover the exciting aromas of whom you have met and where you have been. Watch a cat sitting by an open window scenting the breeze. It will often open its mouth in an expression like a duchess discovering something most distasteful but, in fact, meaning quite the opposite. By increasing the intake of air it increases the information reaching its Jacobson's organ, an olfactory sensor which supplements

Left: *The flexibility of a cat's body, especially its head, enables it to wash everywhere except its head and neck with its scrubbing-brush tongue. It reaches those areas by wetting a paw and 'brushing' with that.*

Right: *The face that looks so appealing to us will look exceedingly menacing to the cat's victim.*

the scent-sensitive cells in the nose. Two ducts lead to this organ from just behind the incisor teeth.

In most mammals smell is the most important sense in locating food and warning of danger but in the cat, as in man and monkey, vision is even more important. A cat's eyes are large and very sensitive. They can see through an angle of 205° and can adapt to a wide range of light intensity, the iris opening to a full circle to admit the greatest possible light under dim conditions and narrowing to a slit when it is bright. The nictitating membrane or 'third eyelid' which rises from the inside corner of the eye can also act as a filter to protect the eye from extremely strong light. Large flat cells form a 'mirror' called the *tapetum lucidum* which reflects light that has not been absorbed in passing through the eye, intensifying the information reaching the retina and enabling a cat to see in conditions which would seem totally dark to most humans. That is why people say that cats can see in the dark, although it is not strictly true as some light must be present. Cats have only one quarter of the sensitivity to colour that we have but it is not true, as was once thought, that they see only in monochrome. They also seem less able to pick out stationary objects or to focus at close quarters but are very quick to notice movement and seem able to judge distances very accurately.

Cats can hear over a range extending from 30 to 45,000 cycles per second – and some even as high as 60,000 – compared with the average human limit of 20,000 cycles (around the top notes of a violin), but comparing ranges does not tell the whole story. For very low notes up to 2,000 cycles, man and cat are about on a par in sensitivity, but for the next 2,000, when our hearing is at its best, the cat excels us, and it is still within its optimum range up to 8,000. The shape of the cat's ears helps to concentrate sound, and the great

Above left: *Out hunting, this Abyssinian keeps down close to the ground and is well concealed by cover. Cats will catch insects, mice and other small rodents, reptiles, and even rabbits.*

Left: *Cats will sometimes spend hours watching caged birds, perhaps because of their tantalising unavailability.*

A bird fancier.

manoeuvrability of ears and head enables it to focus upon the slightest noise and identify its direction. Your cat will hear you turning a street corner long before you reach home, will distinguish the sound of your car's engine from that of every other vehicle and always hear the click as you open the cupboard in which you keep its food.

The cat is also very sensitive to touch. Not only is a large section of the brain devoted to the touch messages from the front paws, but the nose is also very responsive and all over the body are sensitive nerves which respond not only to the direct pressure of objects or animals but to the changes in air pressure caused by their presence. These are most noticeable in the whiskers and the hairs on the back of the forepaws, called vibrissae, and it is by their sensitivity to pressure rather than their width that a cat knows whether it can crawl through a hole. You have quite probably experienced the sensation in the dark of being aware of something blocking your path: the cat has this to a highly developed degree.

Its highly developed senses and efficient physiology equip the cat to be an effective predator. Our pets depend largely upon the food which we give them, but the cat is designed to catch and to kill. Even the domestic cat which has never had to fend for itself will display the skills of the hunter, although it may not associate the kill with food. That knowledge seems not to be instinctive but is taught to kittens by their mother.

Cats are patient hunters. They may wait for hours beside a track along which they expect prey to come, motionless until the moment comes to spring, or they will stalk their quarry stealthily. They like high places from which they can spy out the land, spotting the victim or the enemy or just surveying the scene. They will conceal themselves in deep cover, the spotted and tabby patterns of the wild cats providing excellent camouflage. As they sense the approach of prey, or danger, they concentrate with ears, eyes and nose, gaining as much information as they can. In some instances they may break cover to investigate something more closely, often taking a roundabout route to avoid betraying their presence.

Unless hidden by reliable cover, a cat moves in short, sharp bursts, keeping its body as close to the ground as possible and halting frequently to take stock of the situation. Its ears are flattened to lower its profile as it peers over an obstacle, and its paws are suddenly motionless in mid-air as it freezes to avoid detection. As it closes in on its prey it prepares for its last dash forward, its haunches quivering, partly perhaps from excitement, partly, like an athlete, preparing its muscles for exertion. A cat does not usually leap straight to the kill, but will make a final lunge when it is close to the victim, with its back feet still firmly on the ground to maintain its stability should there be a struggle. The final blow is struck by sinking the incisors into the back of the victim's neck, frequently severing the cervical cord and bringing instant death.

Watch kittens playing with each other, or the way an adult cat stalks a crumpled piece of paper or a cotton reel – or even an imaginary object – and you will see it perform the same manoeuvres as in real hunting except that it will finally grasp the object with its paws instead of imitating the kill. This is typical of the way in which a cat would hunt a rodent or other small animal, except when it waits outside the prey's cover or mouse-hole. In that case it will let the animal get some distance into the open before it springs, so as to avoid the risk of its prey simply diving back into safety again.

The cat's ancestors

The whole cat family is very closely related. From the biggest Siberian Tiger to the smallest domestic tabby they are all identifiably cats and are all classed in the same genera: *Felis*. But zoologists are not absolutely certain from which of the wild cat species our domestic cats are descended. The European Wild Cat, *Felis sylvestris*, looks very like a domestic tabby, and may have played a part, but it seems likely that the relationship with the African Wild Cat, *Felis lybica*, is even closer. This is the cat of northern Africa, and the obvious origin for the cats which were domesticated by the ancient Egyptians: of a group of 192 mummified cats from Egypt unwrapped at the British Museum, four turned out to be the slightly larger Jungle Cat, *Felis chaus*, and all the rest at a halfway stage between the African Wild Cat and the modern domestic cat. *Felis lybica* is found throughout the Middle East and south-western Asia as far as India and there is also a variety or sub-species which differs slightly from this yellow-buff coloured cat.

Unlike the European Wild Cat, the African Wild Cat is comparatively easy to tame, and, although the markings of the European cat are closer to those of the tabby pattern dominant in domestic cats, the African cat, with its rather paler horizontal bands, seems the stronger contender as the domestic cat's progenitor. Some of the ancient Egyptian paintings of cats show coats clearly patterned with stripes and spots. Perhaps the ancient Egyptians chose to domesticate the cats which had the strongest markings.

Outside Africa other species have no doubt contributed to the domestic cat's development: the Spotted Cat in India, for example, and sub-species such as the Indian Desert Cat; *sylvestris, lybica* and their sub-species can all breed with the domestic cat, although it has been claimed that *sylvestris* hybrids prove infertile.

The European Wild Cat is now known only in northern parts of Scotland and more remote parts of Europe, but it once ranged throughout Britain and was common in wooded areas of the European continent. It is usually bigger and more heavily built than the domestic cat and has a larger skull and teeth, but the easiest way to tell a wild cat from a feral tabby is by the rounded end of its tail.

Catching birds requires a different technique, for while the cat is reconnoitring and preparing its attack the bird may well fly off. The effective bird-catcher (and that does not mean all cats) has probably learned to suppress the urge to perform the initial stages of the hunting ritual, and lies in wait until a bird settles within the range of a single spring. Flies and butterflies are usually snatched out of the air between the jaws although some cats will first stun them with a paw. Cats have been known to catch birds in the air, grasping them between their paws. Some cats also learn to fish, hooking their dinner out of a stream with the flick of a paw. A cat will often throw a plaything, or a mouse it has caught, into the air with a similar flicking gesture.

The cat is also well equipped to defend itself. Its spurts of speed over short distances, leaping ability and climbing skill – seeming sometimes to 'bounce' half-way up a wall and take a second spring to the top – enable it to avoid attack, often spitting back its anger from some safe elevation. Cats will not usually seek a serious fight. However, if they are attacked, or required to defend their territory or young, or if competition for a female is extreme, they will attack with the sharp claws of the forepaws and bite, if they can get close enough to the enemy without having their own faces lacerated. Bite-wounds in cat-to-cat fights are rare unless the contestants are ill matched. A cat losing ground will take up an apparently defensive position on its back which brings its powerful hind legs into play – they can deliver a really savage blow – and frees all four sets of claws for action.

An angry cat on the attack is a terrifying spectacle: all teeth and

Opposite: *Keen eyes, sharp ears, pressure and touch sensitive whiskers and sharp canine teeth equip the cat as an efficient nocturnal predator.*

Top left: *A cat will stalk with caution, freezing motionless if it thinks it could be seen by its prey.*

Centre left: *This kitten is obviously playing, but it is in play that it will learn its hunting skills.*

Bottom left: *Covering a fishpond with wire netting may help to protect the fish from hungry, visiting cats.*

claws and flashing eyes. I was once attacked by a previously loving and very gentle cat when I carried into her territory a kitten of which she was already jealous and afraid. I would never have imagined it possible. I threw the kitten to safety and must have kicked the cat away, but not before I had a lacerated hand and a scratched face where teeth and claws had found their mark. A few minutes later, with the intruder shut up in another room, she was licking my wounds and, I am glad to report, she later adopted the kitten as though it were one of her own.

Their physical skills and finely-tuned five senses do not seem enough to explain all the cat's abilities. Have they retained some power that we have lost or perhaps never had? Often a cat, or perhaps some other animal, will seem to react to a presence or a sensation in a room which humans do not register. I have seen two cats both focus on the same non-existent shape and watch it cross before them. Are they seeing into a dimension we cannot explore? Do some cats, like some humans, appear to be psychic? Perhaps there is some totally explicable physical phenomenon, a change of local pressure or temperature, which they have registered but not identified, and their reactions are those of an animal trying to identify the reason for the change rather than a reaction to something outside human comprehension. Since we cannot discover what the cat thinks it saw or heard or felt investigation is almost impossible, but there is evidence of other feline phenomena.

There is 'psi-trailing', for instance, when, as American researchers J. B. Rhine and S. R. Feather describe it, 'an animal, separated from a person or mate to which it has become attached, follows the departed companion into wholly unfamiliar territory and does so at a time and under conditions that would allow the use of no conceivable sensory trail. The distance being long enough, then the animal would have to be guided by a still unrecognized means of knowing . . .', that is to say the distance is too great for the animal to have reached its destination purely by chance.

There are many stories of cats finding their way home from a distance or returning to their old territory when taken away from it and some of these cases are remarkable, but psi-trailing cannot depend upon any identification of a known location as these clearly do, whatever the method used to find it. To be certain that a cat has actually made a psi-trail journey and that it is not just a very similar cat turning up at the new location it is necessary to have some very clear means of identification. Here are some examples which the researchers in parapsychology considered authentic evidence of something inexplicable.

A family moved from California to Oklahoma leaving their cat behind with neighbours, as it had refused to travel in their car. A year and two months later the cat's mistress was in a barn at their new home when a cat jumped through the window on to her shoulder. Surprised, she pushed it off, but yet it felt familiar and on looking at it she saw the cat had the appearance of their former cat. Closer investigation showed that it had a bone deformity that the other cat also had and its behaviour seemed identical. Months later the family

Left: *The darker ticking of the hairs of the Abyssinian's coat is visible here.*

Above right: *The glossy coat of the Havana Cat should be a rich brown rather than black.*

Right: *This moggie may be dozing as he enjoys the warm sunshine, but his ears are pricked and any unusual noise would soon bring him to life.*

with whom the original cat had been left came on a visit and informed them that it had disappeared only two months after the move. Both families were convinced that the two cats were the same animal.

Another cat, missing when the family left Louisiana to move to Texas, turned up in a Texas school-yard five months later, avoiding all the children except the child of the household, whom he allowed to come close and pick him up. The family collie dog and the cat appeared to recognize each other and lay down together as in the past. The cat made growling noises and bit when angry, behaviour it had learned from the dog, and answered to a whistle. It had a scar on one eye that prevented it from closing fully and even a patch of tar on its tail which had been there five months earlier. With so much convincing evidence, identification again seemed to be indisputable.

In another case a cat belonging to a New York vet was left to live in his home area when the vet moved to California. Months later a very similar looking cat walked into his new house, jumped into an armchair and made itself at home. It had a bone deformity on one of the tail vertebrae, identical with one caused by a bite injury in the cat left behind. Could a cat have not only found its way right across a continent but located the very house where its owner now lived? It strains belief, but it seems that this particular cat did.

Understanding your cat

Living with a cat requires a degree of compromise from both you and the animal. If the cat expects you to be its cook, butler, nurse and lavatory attendant as well as universal provider, you have the right to dictate the terms on which you accept the job. Never let any cat get so haughty that it thinks of you as the below-stairs maid. You are the master or mistress and you must establish your authority from the first. Some people succeed in being strict disciplinarians with their animals. I am not one of them though, and perhaps I allow my cats more liberties than you would dream of doing. One of the traits in cats that I find most endearing is their playful wickedness, and if they make a game of trying to break my rules I am as likely to be delighted as annoyed. However, my cats seem to accept that there are two layers to domestic discipline, and behaviour permitted within the family is barred when there are visitors – although not all cats may understand the distinction.

Discipline, both for your convenience and the cat's good, should start early and must be consistent. Most cats are quick to learn, if not always to obey. Considerable restraint on your part may be necessary to ignore the persistent, plaintive appeals of a cat, especially a kitten, to be permitted a relaxation of regulations, but harden your heart for, given an inch, a cat will almost certainly take a mile! Be firm but gentle: punishments should not come into training. Admonishment with a severe tone of voice, or at most a light tap on the flanks or on the nose, should be the strongest reproof. Never strike cats severely, as they bruise easily and your blows may prove quite painful. A cat will certainly remember

Left: Cats are usually extremely tolerant of children. Lasting friendships are frequently formed between them.

a blow but not the reason for it and will probably distrust you.

Try not to use the cat's name when rebuking it, so that when you call it, its name will have only happy associations. Choose a name which you can call clearly and which is easily recognized. Use it, or a whistle, or some other signal when it is feeding time and it will soon learn to answer to the call. If it is so busily engaged in other, more important enterprises that it blatantly ignores you, that does not mean it has not understood, simply that you do not have the same priorities!

The rules you make will be up to you. Certain parts of your home may be out of bounds or you may object to the cat jumping on to tables or shelving. You may forbid feeding, or asking for titbits, when the family are at meals. If you don't want the cat to jump up, you just have to lift it down, harshly saying 'Bad cat' or something similar. Watch for it thinking of doing the same again, and reprove it as you see it about to jump. Eventually you will win, but do not be so sure that the cat will stay on the ground in your absence. If a cat pesters for food at table ignore it. If it reaches up with its paws push it down. Do not weaken!

Scratching on furniture or curtains and covers can be corrected if you have a scratching post. Pick the cat up whenever it starts to scratch, carry it to the post, stretch out its forepaws and dig its claws into the covering on the post. Repeat this whenever it scratches elsewhere, or reprove it when you see it about to scratch, and carry it to the post. Cats do not like to do something that draws reproof and will soon give it up, unless they are feeling ignored or wronged, in which case they will often deliberately do things to annoy you.

Some training is necessary for the cat's own benefit. Leaping on to surfaces which are likely to become hot – whether hotplates on a cooker or the top of an oil stove – must be forbidden. There is no way in which the cat on floor level can tell if a higher surface is safe. Once a cat has burned itself it is unlikely to jump up again, but burns can be very serious, and learning by experience is best avoided. Scalds are another common injury: make allowances for a cat weaving between your feet when you are carrying a pan of hot water, or better still, teach the cat not to pester you in such circumstances, but to wait patiently for its own food, as what you are cooking is not coming its way!

Electric cables must also be taboo. If you play with your cat with moving pieces of string it should not be very difficult to train it not to touch immobile cables, but avoid hanging wires from tables wherever possible so that the cat is not misled. Chewing through a cable can easily give the cat a shock. If a cat is electrocuted, switch off the current immediately. If this is impossible, make sure that you are well insulated before touching anything. Wear rubber gloves and stand on a rubber mat or some other non-conductive material, or at least wear rubber-soled shoes, and if you touch the animal with bare hands ensure that no other part of your body is in contact with the floor or you may carry current through you to earth. Many animals urinate as one of the reactions to electrocution; urine can conduct electricity, so avoid the puddle until the power is switched off. Immediate treatment for electrocution is artificial respiration. Electric shock can also cause heart failure and if the cable has been chewed the mouth may be burned. Veterinary help should be sought immediately.

Training a cat requires time and patience and an understanding of the cat's nature and behaviour. A cat is a carnivore; it may be possible to feed it on non-animal protein, and vegetarian animal foods are available in some places, but you should not blame the cat if it prefers the diet for which its digestive system was designed. A cat is a hunter; if it catches small animals and birds it is only following years of instinct. You may be able to train a cat not to bring its kill to you, or not to attack in your presence but it may revert to type when your back is turned and it would be very ungallant of you to spurn the gift of prey.

Right: *All cats will sit quietly for long periods of time, watching the world.*

Below: *Some kittens find it difficult to work out reflections particularly when they first encounter them.*

If cats live where it is impossible for them to hunt, or are firmly dissuaded from it, they must be given a substitute activity or they may become frustrated. My own cats rarely have the opportunity to catch anything more exciting than an insect, but they expend a lot of energy beating an oversized toy mouse with their hind feet, chasing after string or fabric belts which perhaps stir some genetic memory of snake-like prey, pouncing on anything that moves, battling with newspapers and retrieving balls of screwed up paper as brightly as any gundog: and most of these games require considerable human participation.

Watch the games that kittens play with each other and with their mother. Roles constantly change, the chaser suddenly becomes the chased, and play restrains the release of real aggression. It is interesting to note how rolling upon the back is often an invitation to a game, and how the sound of movement attracts attention. In the same way that the rustle in the undergrowth alerts the hunter to its prey, so, for a cat confined indoors, the sound of a piece of paper being crumpled leads a cat to expect you to initiate a game.

In kittens' play there is a distinct pattern of behaviour for relationships with signals which you should learn to interpret when they are displayed to you. Most people will be familiar with the image of a cat with bristling fur and high-arched back, apparently angry and defiant, but this posture is not as simple as it at first appears. It is a combination of both aggressive and submissive gestures. To make itself more frightening to an enemy, or to threaten an intruder, a cat will increase its size by making its fur stand erect, it may open its mouth to show its dangerous teeth and perhaps spit defiance while its ears are flattened (less easy to bite or claw than if they remained pricked). A submissive cat, on the contrary, will make itself as small as possible and probably back away. The arched back is a combination of the two: despite the aggressive bristling the front legs do not carry the cat forward to attack but at best stand their ground, perhaps even retreat, while the rear end, more confident, moves forward and pushes the back upwards. Cats will often hold this pose when they meet on a

disputed right of way, spitting and snarling, as each tries to out-countenance the other. Eventually one submits or the confrontation ends in battle between the two.

Cats do not go looking for fights, except for fun, and they give plenty of warning of the state of their emotions. Ears, eyes, tail, fur, voice, their whole body, signal their increasing anger, fear or pleasure: it does not require any great interpretative skill to understand them. In fact I do not think it is anthropomorphic to suggest that their signals are very like human ones. Pleading, warning, threatening, the cat's voice gets gradually louder if it is subjected to treatment it dislikes. Its eyes will change from hurt to rage. A hunched crouch shows its terror, quite different from the confidently comfortable, normal way of sitting. A sprawled-out body and an exposed belly show its feeling of security and relaxation. Its ears show its alertness, apprehension, concentration and exasperation. The more perked up and pointed forward they are, the more intense is its interest, and the

more they are pressed back and down, the more wary you should be.

The tail is another indicator of mood. Held gaily aloft it shows the cat's confidence. Fluffed up like a Christmas tree it is an instant reaction to an apparent threat. High and fluffed it reflects the cat's belligerence, fluffed and dragging it shows its fear.

Purring has never been properly explained. All we really know is that cats purr when they are contented. We do not even know whether it is made consciously or is completely involuntary. It has been claimed that there is a very deep purr made by some cats when they are in pain. Very young kittens purr and the sound may be a signal to their mother to release milk: perhaps the way in which cats often purr in friendly greeting is an 'infantile signal' which is retained in adulthood for a different purpose.

Above: *This Blue kitten is approaching the adult with confidence, although the white cat's ear position suggests that it will not put up with any nonsense.*

Right: *The white kitten is plainly frightened and is actually retreating.*

This seems very likely, for a happy cat will often knead a person who is holding it, pushing with its paws, stretching and contracting its toes, in just the way it kneads its mother's nipples to increase the flow of milk, and it may even suck and salivate as though it were actually being fed.

Many of the actions we make in fondling a cat, scratching behind the ears or under the chin, and massaging, are obviously pleasant to the cats themselves, and the general stroking and caressing motions must be very like those made by its mother when it was a kitten, to keep it clean and encourage its digestive system to operate. Although mutual grooming is a gesture which adult cats and many other animals exchange, it is also a reflection of maternal care which indicates relaxation and friendship. Perhaps its continual availability from humans helps to keep the cat from 'growing up'; indeed, pets that get a great deal of attention and do not have the normal adult cares of providing for themselves seem to retain the playfulness of the juvenile.

Cats will often invent their own games and turn not only the usual piece of string, cotton reel or ping-pong ball into playthings, but a kitchen sponge, a pencil, or an old sock. A thin plastic sponge can be thrown, chased and caught and, because its flight is unpredictable, may provide much fun – but do not allow kittens or any cat which tries to chew them to play with such materials. They can easily become lodged in the throat or stomach. There is a wide range of cat toys sold by pet suppliers: toy mice, spiders dangling on springs, open-sided plastic balls which the cat can hook up with a claw as well as hit and kick, even a little house with a mouse inside which can be hooked out and jumps back in again as soon as it is released.

A cat will play many games on its own, but with another cat as a playfellow it can extend its repertoire, and if you join in there will be fun for both of you. Most cats respond to playful overtures and always appreciate an audience for their skills. Some cats will play with anyone, others prefer particular partners for certain games. I had one cat that would play retrieving games, taking a ball of crumpled paper to members of the household in turn for each to throw. One pair of cats seemed to have an agreement that one had the prior right to string games and the other to ball games, and that each should play them alone for several minutes before the other joined it.

Cats love pouncing upon anything that continues to appear and disappear, whether it is a pencil poked beneath a newspaper, a finger underneath the bedclothes or your toes beneath a dressing gown. Most cats are very careful to sheathe their claws when playing with humans – one sibling pair I had would jump upon my bare shoulders without a claw protruding, although when I was fully clothed they would sink their claws well into my jacket. However, young kittens frequently cannot sheathe their claws, and if an older cat gets very excited during a rough game something may suddenly trigger play into aggression. If you play fighting games with a cat or let it pounce on your bare fingers you would be wise to wear gloves: if you know the cat well you should be

able to recognize the signs of mounting excitement and know when to stop. Jumping in and out of cardboard boxes, scurrying beneath sheets of newspaper and diving into paper bags are frequently favourite diversions for cats; they like somewhere to hide and may enjoy playing hide and seek.

One tom of mine (who took so little care in hiding that I usually had to pretend I had not seen him) was so eager to be discovered that if more than a few moments elapsed he would call out where he was or even half emerge to speed up his discovery. When it was my turn to hide I could never be quite sure whether he was just a little slow-witted or whether he in turn deliberately pretended, again, not to be able to find me.

That particular cat was immensely patient, and would sit for hours beside a piece of string, waiting for me to pick it up and start a game, a quite obvious request, but there were many other ways in which we seemed to communicate with each other. He was particularly sensitive to emotional strain and would respond with a great display of affection; if I hit a problem at the typewriter he would jump on to my lap, distracting me for a moment so that I could return to work with my mind cleared to tackle the problem afresh. I always seemed to know what he wanted too, more so than with any other cat, but it was not merely a matter of translating 'cat language'. Perhaps, just as an animal recognizes all those tiny actions which precede a major one, such as packing before going away or the small habitual movements that signal whether you are going to the cupboard or the door, I too had unconsciously become responsive to a whole range of his signals. I think it is something which we can all develop in a close relationship with an animal, not by sitting down and trying to work out every possible signal (fascinating though that would be) but by giving the animal sufficient time and attention for it to happen.

Cats like a very regular life, and if you establish a fixed timetable they will keep to it. They will usually learn to allow for such regular occurrences as the Sunday lie-in. One cat I knew used to savage a pair of very expensive hi-fi speakers each Sunday morning until its owners satisfied its needs and then went back to bed with the Sunday papers. One American cat always knew when it was Monday and (yes, it is true) regularly came home early for

Top right: *A harness is safer and more comfortable for a cat than a collar, but do not leave it on when the cat is roaming on its own; the harness could too easily catch on any projection.*

Right: *Pushing open a door is something most cats become adept at themselves, although this can result in their being inadvertently shut in!*

Good luck – bad luck

Some British and American superstitions
Black cats are lucky – in England
White cats are lucky – in America and many European countries.
It is lucky to own a black cat but unlucky to meet one – in parts of Yorkshire.

If a cat crosses your path, stroke it three times for good luck.

If it runs away you will have bad luck.

If a black cat crosses your path, take off your hat and turn it round in a complete circle and you will avoid bad luck.

If a cat sneezes three times the whole household will get colds.
If a cat sneezes near her mistress on her wedding morning the marriage will be a happy one.

A three-colour cat prevents fires.

You will always be lucky if you know how to make friends with strange cats.

If a strange white cat comes to your home unwelcome guests will follow.

If a cat follows you along the street you will have money coming to you.

It is particularly lucky if a grey cat walks across your path.

A scratch from a cat is an indication of disappointment to come.

his dinner on that day, set off at 7.45 to cross at a traffic light and made his way to a window ledge where he settled down to watch a weekly game of bingo. We do not know what pleasure he got from it. The person who reported the story suggested he was there 'to see and hear the human species gamble and scream'.

The behaviour of its owner provides the cat with plenty of information; signs that the normal pattern of events will not be followed may give a cat a very good idea of what is going to happen, but it may not agree to accept the modification and will protest. Scratching or other minor misdemeanours are not unusual in such circumstances. A persistent refusal to consider the cat's wishes, or even being away from home rather more frequently than the cat would like, may lead to the rather

more troublesome breakdown of house-training as a protest, but failure to use a litter tray and soiling in the house is much more likely to be a simple indication that the cat is rather more fastidious than you are and thinks the tray should be changed more frequently!

Cats are generally scrupulously clean in their behaviour. One ill cat which was vomiting frequently, quickly appreciated that I would rush in with a piece of newspaper if I saw it about to be sick and would seek out a place where there was already paper by its litter tray, rush to the nearest newspaper on a table, or at least would make sure that it was on a smooth piece of tile or wooden floor and not on a carpet. This was not training but the cat's own observation: it must have realized that I showed greater effort and

Above: *Kittens should be allowed to explore new surroundings at their own pace. This Tabby Colourpoint is making sure that the flowerbeds are safe places in which to play and roam.*

perhaps more agitation in clearing up a carpet.

Most cats will accept your rules, especially if they are accompanied by particular privileges. Then they will sit quietly at mealtimes, if there is a guarantee of a morsel for them as soon as the humans get down from table. Even so, my cats will do something to attract attention to their good behaviour! Some cats have gone much further: if they feel that they are being ignored, they not only break rules by jumping on to out-of-bound surfaces but deliberately and methodically knock objects on to the floor. One neutered tom (the one that so liked playing hide-and-seek)

89

would do things that led to reproof and punishment just to get attention. He would rather have a spanking than be ignored.

Some cats seem to sit upon the open pages of a book or push against your newspaper whenever you settle down to read, to win your attention. With patience they can be induced to sit quietly upon your lap instead.

Cats do like to share things with you. Some will join their humans for a walk, and most kittens can be taught to wear a lead. First they must be accustomed to wearing a collar, but if they are not allowed out on their own, a harness would be better, and more comfortable for the lead will not then pull on the neck. I have to admit that I have not been very successful at training cats to leads. You must start when they are very young and be very patient. Persist, however little success you feel you may be having and perhaps the breakthrough will come. I wish you luck!

The nearest I came to success was with a cat that had been born and reared in a flat and lived with me in a block of flats. It had never been outdoors on its own and, intriguing though the excitements of the world outside might be, it felt more confident if it stayed close to me. Although it thoroughly enjoyed seeing the world from the safety of a car, or even from a bus or underground train, it would freeze at the kerb and refuse to cross a road, even when there was no immediate traffic passing, and would have to be carried across.

Above: *Cats love jumping and climbing. Given a garden with walls and trees they will find plenty to amuse themselves.*

Left: *A cat looks down confidently from its tree-top perch, knowing the descent will present no problem.*

Before attaching a leather lead use a light nylon one or a piece of string, to get the kitten used to having something there. Young kittens have a strong instinct to follow their mother, and you are mother substitute. When the kitten has accepted the presence of the 'lead', take hold of the other end and, with the cord slack, call the kitten to you, drawing in the lead as it approaches. Now try walking with the cat on the lead. The cat will probably sit still and refuse to budge but eventually will walk a few steps. Do not press it for more. Next day try again: perhaps it will walk a little further. Keep the lead slack at first; when the kitten is completely used to it, allow it to pull taut and restrain the cat's movements. It may take many sessions to get even this far, but always remember that a few minutes' daily practice is much more productive than half an hour once a week. Lessons should never last so long that the cat dislikes them.

It is most important for your cat to trust you. Do not try to deceive it. If you have to give it a pill, let it be aware of the fact but follow the pill-giving with a favourite game, or if it is ill and not up to playing, reward it with plenty of praise and attention. You can pit your wits against each

Weather cats and seafarers

In Japan, where tortoiseshell and tri-coloured cats are thought most lucky, sailors used to believe that if a tortoiseshell cat climbed to the top of the mast it could drive storm devils away.

In Malaya and Indonesia people believed that bathing a cat would bring rain.

Throwing a cat overboard will raise a storm.

If a sailor's wife keeps a black cat her husband will come safely home.

Sicilian sailors believed that if the ship's cat miaowed while they were saying the rosary at departure the voyage would be a boring one.

If a cat sits with its back to the fire, look out for a frost.

other so long as you both know that you are playing, and are never vindictive. If your cat knows that it can trust you completely it will even let you do things that it dislikes because it somehow knows that you are doing them for its own benefit. Almost all cats are immensely tolerant of children, who will often accidentally mishandle them, and they extend this tolerance to trusted adults, giving ample warning before they take any action to defend themselves. However, if a cat has been badly treated at some earlier time, this kind of trust may prove very difficult to establish.

The way you handle a cat is important. Unless you already have its total confidence – and then only when it knows that you are playing – never approach a cat with loud noises or snatch at it. Stroke it and say hello before you try to pick it up. A kitten can be lifted by the scruff of the neck, in the same way that its mother carries it, but an adult cat should always be supported beneath the body and transferred into the crook of the arm for carrying. To restrain a cat, grip it by the scruff and, when lifting it, grip its rear paws from the back so that you can support its weight upon the forearm that is holding them.

Always impress upon children that a cat is not a toy and can be injured easily if not handled gently.

Left: *This quizzical cat is clearly waiting to see what your next move will be before he makes his!*

Notice the way in which a friendly cat approaches you. It will probably give you a chirrupy vocal greeting, its head raised to you and its tail gaily held upright with the tip waving. It will rub against your legs or, if you bend down to stroke it, against your hand. A louder purr as you reach its level is more than a friendship gesture. As the cat rubs its cheeks against you it is actually marking you with its scent. It is identifying you as friend, if not a possession, just as an un-neutered tom marks out his territory by spraying urine and the product of his scent glands. Think how easily your palms can sweat: as you stroke the cat you too are 'marking' it by your action.

Cats are very possessive about their territory. In areas where many cats live and their paths must cross they will often wait to make sure that another cat is clear before using a common route. They may have many feline friends, but they will be very selective about which one they will allow into their home area. They may claim a whole garden as private, or it may be just a chair. With cats living together there may be only a limited privacy: I had a cat which always insisted that my bed was his domain, but his sister was allowed to join him provided that he took up position first and she approached with deference and washed him before settling down. Some cats, Siamese in particular, may be even more possessive about people than they are about places, and will show considerable jealousy and pique

if their human gives too much attention to another cat.

Perhaps one reason why the cat accepts the rules we impose in our homes is that it acknowledges our territory. One kitten joined me when I was sharing a large flat. It acknowledged me as proprietor of the place and also accepted that the young lady who shared it with me was already resident and therefore had territorial claims and could issue orders. The kitten and she became good friends. It was the time of the maxi-skirt and whenever she came home the kitten would run up the length of her coat and sit upon her shoulder to greet her. She fed the kitten if I was not home, but when I moved into a house, although she was a frequent visitor and the cat remained good friends with her, her authority was lost. If she administered reproof the cat would argue back, as if to say 'This isn't your house, you can't tell me what to do. This is my territory!' Even when I was away on business or on holiday and my former flat-mate moved in to look after my cats, she still was not acknowledged as boss, although they were dependent upon her for food, games and everything they needed.

Study your cats and learn to communicate with them. It requires no effort, just a little time and attention. The more you understand them, the better you will be able to care for them and keep them happy, and the greater the pleasure you will get from sharing your life with them.

Index

Acknowledgments

The publishers would like to thank the following organizations and individuals for their kind permission to reproduce the photographs in this book:

Animal Graphics: 2–3; Ardea London: (Andre Fatras) 8–9, (Jean Paul Ferrero) 36, 61; Barnaby's Picture Library: 52–53; Sdeuard C Bisserot: 39, 66; Peter Clayton: 10; Bruce Coleman: (Hans Reinhard) 1, 6–7, 23, 42, 58–59; Anne Cumbers: 20, 32, 37 centre right, 38, 40, 41, 44, 45 above right, 46–47, 48 below, 49, 55, 62–63, 67 above right, 68 above left, 70 below *left, 71, 79 above left, 81 above left, 88 above and below right, 89; Daily Telegraph Colour Library: (Robert Hallmann) 33; C M Dixon: 48 above left; Robert Estall: 53 below right, 78; Mary Evans Picture Library: 15, 16, 76 below left; Sonia Halliday Photographs: 43 below left, centre and right; Jacana Agence de Presse: Endpapers, 22, 80; William MacQuitty: 9 below right; Margaret McLean: 30, 37 above right, 88 below left; The Mansell Collection: 14; Jane Miller: 27 below right, 84; John Moss: 24 below left 54 above and below right, 56, 65 below left and right, 67 above left; Pete Myers – photo (Private Collection): 13; Rex Features: 75;* *Clive Sawyer: 81 below; Tony Stone Associates: 17, 28, 60, 90–91, 92; Sally Anne Thompson: 4–5, 26–27, 47 above right, 63 above right, 68–69, 72–73, 74, 76 above left, 79 centre; Transworld Feature Syndicate: 79 below left; Jerry Tubby: 35, 86; Bavaria Verlag: 82–83, (Hans Reinhard) 11, (Klaus Frerichs) 24 below right, (H Bielfeld) 37 below right, (U Kment) 85; Welbeck Abbey: 70 above left; Shin Yoshino: 12, 19 above right, 21 centre, 25, 64, 68 below left and right, 73 above right, 87, 91 above right; Zefa: 29, 45 below right, 50–51, 93; Zefa/Reinhard: 18–19, 21 above right, 31, 57, 77, 94.*